# U.S. COUNTERNARCOTICS OPERATIONS IN AFGHANISTAN

## HEARING

BEFORE THE

### SUBCOMMITTEE ON
### THE MIDDLE EAST AND NORTH AFRICA

OF THE

## COMMITTEE ON FOREIGN AFFAIRS
## HOUSE OF REPRESENTATIVES

ONE HUNDRED THIRTEENTH CONGRESS

SECOND SESSION

FEBRUARY 5, 2014

## Serial No. 113–120

Printed for the use of the Committee on Foreign Affairs

Available via the World Wide Web: http://www.foreignaffairs.house.gov/ or
http://www.gpo.gov/fdsys/

U.S. GOVERNMENT PRINTING OFFICE

86–589PDF        WASHINGTON : 2014

For sale by the Superintendent of Documents, U.S. Government Printing Office
Internet: bookstore.gpo.gov   Phone: toll free (866) 512–1800; DC area (202) 512–1800
Fax: (202) 512–2104   Mail: Stop IDCC, Washington, DC 20402–0001

## COMMITTEE ON FOREIGN AFFAIRS

EDWARD R. ROYCE, California, *Chairman*

CHRISTOPHER H. SMITH, New Jersey
ILEANA ROS-LEHTINEN, Florida
DANA ROHRABACHER, California
STEVE CHABOT, Ohio
JOE WILSON, South Carolina
MICHAEL T. McCAUL, Texas
TED POE, Texas
MATT SALMON, Arizona
TOM MARINO, Pennsylvania
JEFF DUNCAN, South Carolina
ADAM KINZINGER, Illinois
MO BROOKS, Alabama
TOM COTTON, Arkansas
PAUL COOK, California
GEORGE HOLDING, North Carolina
RANDY K. WEBER SR., Texas
SCOTT PERRY, Pennsylvania
STEVE STOCKMAN, Texas
RON DeSANTIS, Florida
DOUG COLLINS, Georgia
MARK MEADOWS, North Carolina
TED S. YOHO, Florida
LUKE MESSER, Indiana

ELIOT L. ENGEL, New York
ENI F.H. FALEOMAVAEGA, American
  Samoa
BRAD SHERMAN, California
GREGORY W. MEEKS, New York
ALBIO SIRES, New Jersey
GERALD E. CONNOLLY, Virginia
THEODORE E. DEUTCH, Florida
BRIAN HIGGINS, New York
KAREN BASS, California
WILLIAM KEATING, Massachusetts
DAVID CICILLINE, Rhode Island
ALAN GRAYSON, Florida
JUAN VARGAS, California
BRADLEY S. SCHNEIDER, Illinois
JOSEPH P. KENNEDY III, Massachusetts
AMI BERA, California
ALAN S. LOWENTHAL, California
GRACE MENG, New York
LOIS FRANKEL, Florida
TULSI GABBARD, Hawaii
JOAQUIN CASTRO, Texas

AMY PORTER, *Chief of Staff*    THOMAS SHEEHY, *Staff Director*
JASON STEINBAUM, *Democratic Staff Director*

————

## SUBCOMMITTEE ON THE MIDDLE EAST AND NORTH AFRICA

ILEANA ROS-LEHTINEN, Florida, *Chairman*

STEVE CHABOT, Ohio
JOE WILSON, South Carolina
ADAM KINZINGER, Illinois
TOM COTTON, Arkansas
RANDY K. WEBER SR., Texas
RON DeSANTIS, Florida
DOUG COLLINS, Georgia
MARK MEADOWS, North Carolina
TED S. YOHO, Florida
LUKE MESSER, Indiana

THEODORE E. DEUTCH, Florida
GERALD E. CONNOLLY, Virginia
BRIAN HIGGINS, New York
DAVID CICILLINE, Rhode Island
ALAN GRAYSON, Florida
JUAN VARGAS, California
BRADLEY S. SCHNEIDER, Illinois
JOSEPH P. KENNEDY III, Massachusetts
GRACE MENG, New York
LOIS FRANKEL, Florida

# CONTENTS

# U.S. COUNTERNARCOTICS OPERATIONS IN AFGHANISTAN

---

## WEDNESDAY, FEBRUARY 5, 2014

House of Representatives,
Subcommittee on the Middle East and North Africa,
Committee on Foreign Affairs,
*Washington, DC.*

The committee met, pursuant to notice, at 2 o'clock p.m., in room 2172 Rayburn House Office Building, Hon. Ileana Ros-Lehtinen (chairman of the subcommittee) presiding.

Ms. Ros-Lehtinen. The subcommittee will come to order because you have been patiently awaiting us for a while, and Mr. Cicilline is coming right on cue.

After recognizing myself and the ranking member, Ted Deutch, for 5 minutes each for our opening statements, I will then recognize other members seeking recognition for 1 minute each.

We will then hear from our witnesses, and without objection the witnesses' prepared statements will be made a part of the record, and members may have 5 days in which to insert statements and questions for the record subject to the length limitation in the rules.

The Chair recognizes herself for 5 minutes.

Since Fiscal Year 2002, the U.S. has appropriated almost $7.5 billion for counternarcotics efforts in Afghanistan. This funding includes over $4 billion for the Department of State's Bureau of International Narcotics and Law Enforcement Affairs, INL; nearly $3 billion for the Department of Defense Drug Interdiction and Counter Drug activities, and just over $200 million for the Drug Enforcement Administration, DEA. This amounts to about 7 percent of the $102 billion the U.S. has appropriated for relief and reconstruction in Afghanistan over that period of time.

Last year alone we allocated nearly $1 billion toward these counternarcotics efforts. This is a significant amount of U.S. taxpayer money, and it is extremely important that this subcommittee continue to conduct its oversight role to ensure that we are achieving our goals and objectives, and that this money is being properly spent.

Yet, despite all of this money being spent, 2013 was a record-breaking year in terms of poppy cultivation in Afghanistan. Afghanistan produced over 80 percent of the world's opium last year, and the illegal drug trade is a contributing factor to many of the major challenges facing Afghanistan and the U.S. The drug trade helps to generate hundreds of millions of dollars for the Taliban and other extremist groups every year. It creates an increase in corruption, and it creates a very serious public health challenge in Afghanistan as more and more Afghans get addicted to the readily available drugs.

The narco-terrorism connection is particularly troubling given the vast sums of money extremist groups can extract from the drug trade and to fund terrorist activities against the United States and our interests worldwide. And the money drug trafficking generates permeates its way through all levels of government, as corruption and drug trafficking in Afghanistan go hand in hand.

Last May, I led a codel to Afghanistan and had Foreign Affairs Committee colleagues, Mr. Kennedy and Dr. Bera along, and we had the opportunity to see firsthand the work that the INL, DoD, and the DEA are doing on the counternarcotics front, and get briefed by the folks on the ground about the current situation. We also visited the DEA Center in Afghanistan, and it was quite impressive to see their operations and how their programs are run.

I commend these brave men and women for doing their absolute best to fight this very serious problems with their resources.

The amount of capacity-building, specialty training, and information sharing that INL, DoD, and DEA have done is a testament to their commitment to aggressively fight this threat. And though there have been great strides made, I remain worried about the future of counternarcotics efforts in Afghanistan as we approach the 2014 withdrawal with even greater uncertainty.

All of our counternarcotics efforts in Afghanistan to this point have relied heavily on a robust U.S. military presence. To add insult to injury, Karzai has not been willing to provide vital resources to help the eradication teams in Afghanistan. As a result of the U.S. drawdown, many of our operations have had to be scaled back, and we have reduced our counternarcotics presence in Afghanistan in conjunction with the dwindling number of troops. And now with the post-2014 U.S. footprint still in doubt, we are making it even more difficult for these agencies that will have to make corresponding decreases in their enduring presence and to make adjustments to their operations.

I'm concerned that because DEA personnel is being scaled back by over 70 percent, our counternarcotics efforts will be undermined and will not be successful.

As Ambassador Brownfield notes in his testimony, these counternarcotics efforts do not take place in a vacuum. Addressing the drug issue in Afghanistan is a key part of our overall strategy for Afghanistan and for the overall war on terror. So much attention has been given to the Bilateral Security Agreement, the upcoming elections in April, and the mercurial nature of Karzai that we must not lose sight of the counternarcotics threat that poses a direct threat to our national security and the regional stability.

And now I'd be glad to turn to Mr. Cicilline for any opening statements that he would like to make.

Mr. CICILLINE. Thank you, Madam Chair. Thank you, Chairman Ros-Lehtinen and Ranking Member Deutch for holding today's hearing on this very important issue.

As we continue drawing down combat operations in Afghanistan it's increasingly the responsibility of the Afghan people to operate, build, and maintain their own civilian and military capacity. The United States has built an important foundation for Afghanistan's future, but long-term stability and a sustainable peace in the region can only be accomplished when the people of Afghanistan take on these responsibilities.

Unfortunately, ongoing and prevalent narcotics activity in Afghanistan has led to aggressive momentum in many areas, narcotics activities correlated with political and economic instability, and has a substantial effect on the quality of life. The United States must continue to monitor counternarcotics efforts in Afghanistan to determine how U.S. interests may be best served as we transition our combat forces out of the country.

I look forward to hearing the perspectives of the witnesses we have assembled to discuss U.S. counternarcotics efforts in Afghanistan, and how they will shape our relationship going forward.

And with that, I'd like to yield the balance of my time to our ranking member, Mr. Deutch.

Ms. ROS-LEHTINEN. Well, thank you so much, Mr. Cicilline. And we are pleased to give the time to Mr. Deutch to make his opening statement, and then we will turn to Mr. Brooks for a minute statement, et cetera. Thank you.

Mr. DEUTCH. Thank you, Madam Chairman, and I thank my friend from Rhode Island. And thanks, Madam Chairman, for holding this hearing.

While most of our discussions about Afghanistan are focused on troop numbers and reconciliation talks, counternarcotics is an issue that's going to play a significant role in shaping Afghanistan's long-term future. Afghanistan's narcotics trade has been a financial boon for the insurgency in Afghanistan as the world's number one producer of opium providing 80 percent of the world's heroin supply. Afghan drugs make their way to Russia, to Europe, and just over the border to Iran where the drug addiction rate is the highest in the world.

The illicit drug trade in Afghanistan accounts for close to half of the Taliban's budget. The undeniable link between drug money and terrorism funding means that this isn't just an Afghan threat, it is an international security threat.

For many years, U.S. efforts to combat the illicit Afghan drug trade focus on poppy eradication, but the emphasis on eradication did little to actually alleviate the drug production problem. The focus on eradication instead left rural farmers without a steady income and more vulnerable to the law of extremism or other black market economic activities, but economic opportunity and security go hand in hand. Programs to replace poppies with alternative crops won't succeed unless there is a more holistic approach. Simply giving farmers what seeds to plant in lieu of poppies won't do anything if Afghan wheat has not been marketed as a viable option to importers. Efforts to improve Afghanistan's agriculture exports will only decrease the desire for Afghan farmers to cultivate the poppy. They'll strengthen Afghanistan's legitimate economy instead of propping up the black market drug trade.

Programs like the Hellman Food Zone, a comprehensive effort funded by the U.S., Britain, and Denmark not only established alternative crops, but provided for crop storage and overland shipping routes out of the province. That's seeing success, and I hope we have success replicating these efforts in Kandahar and elsewhere around the country.

I know that many see the rise in poppy cultivation as an indicator that counternarcotics operations have failed, but we have, in fact, seen real and serious progress in many of our joint counternarcotics programs, most notably interdiction efforts with DEA as the lead law enforcement agency have led to vetted and trained units of counternarcotics police of Afghanistan.

As Mr. Capra will explain in his testimony, these units have led to close to 2,500 operations that resulted in over 2,200 arrests in the past 9 months. This is a good news story.

Narcotics trade and terrorism funding go hand in hand across the globe, and I commend the DEA's activities to combat this worldwide, but in a country as frail as Afghanistan, and as fragile as Afghanistan is, the security risks from propping up insurgents with hundreds of millions of dollars to fund their operations can't be overstated.

The United States trained and supported Counternarcotics Justice Center heard 700 drug cases last year, but without proper support from the Afghan Government, the CNJC has largely prosecuted low-level couriers.

I commend Ambassador Brownfield and his team, and INL for the work that they've done to support efforts to go after high-level traffickers which resulted in the successful prosecution and incarceration of a U.S. designated drug kingpin, but the fact remains the United States alone cannot stop the Afghan drug trade. We can provide the Afghan Government with the necessary training and support, but no amount of funding can provide the political will to aggressively confront all aspects of drug production and trafficking.

I do believe that there are elements of the Afghan Government deeply committed to counternarcotics. The Minister of Counternarcotics said last month that there is a need for severe punishment of traffickers, adding, ''I hope that in 2014 we will witness a declining trend in both cultivation and production of opium.'' So, as we look ahead to the future of U.S. operations in Afghanistan, we have to turn our focus to ways to help the Afghans sustain the counternarcotics regime that we have helped them build.

What can we do to insure that the programs we have worked so hard to build from the Afghan Counternarcotics Police, to the prosecutors of the Counternarcotics Justice Center, and the staff of the hundred drug treatment centers, what can we do to help those continue to function with a decreased U.S. presence? And how can we ensure that our reduced security operations don't stretch the Afghan security forces so thin that counternarcotics simply becomes an afterthought.

The U.S. has never conducted counternarcotics operations of this scale in a war zone, and I commend our witnesses for the work that your agencies have done in a most challenging environment. I look forward to hearing from each of you, and I yield back.

Ms. ROS-LEHTINEN. Amen. Thank you so much. Mr. Cotton, we're pleased to hear from you. Okay. Mr. Weber.

Mr. WEBER. I'm going to follow the Senator's lead.

Ms. ROS-LEHTINEN. Okay, let me see. Who's there next to you? Mr. Collins. Oh, boy, oh, boy, pithy, very pithy.

Mr. COTTON. We've kept the witnesses waiting long enough.

Ms. ROS-LEHTINEN. Okay, thank you. Ms. Meng here? Thank you.

Ms. MENG. Don't worry, mine is brief. Thank you, Madam Chairwoman and Ranking Member Deutch for holding this important hearing. Thank you to our witnesses for being here today, as well.

U.S. operations in Afghanistan are critical to the security of the United States, especially now that our decade long military presence will be decreasing. Concentrating on counternarcotics operations is essential. Afghanistan remains the world's primary source of opium poppy cultivation and has a large hand in drug production and distribution.

Drug trafficking funnels money into terrorist groups and contributes to economic and political instability. The drug trade in Afghanistan threatens not only the country itself, but also the entire Middle East region and the United States. Therefore, I'm very interested in how the U.S. can sustain and improve its counternarcotics operations in Afghanistan. I look forward to hearing from today's panelists from the Departments of State, Justice, and Defense about this serious problem. Thank you.

Ms. ROS-LEHTINEN. Thank you, Ms. Meng. My Florida colleague, Ms. Frankel, is recognized.

Ms. FRANKEL. Thank you, Madam Chair. Thank you for this hearing, and thank you to the witnesses for being here. And I will listen with great interest and reserve my questions.

Ms. ROS-LEHTINEN. Thank you, ma'am. And Mr. Connolly is recognized.

Mr. CONNOLLY. Well, Madam Chairwoman, as you know, I served on the Senate Foreign Relations Committee many years ago where I looked at the drug problem. I have to say it's deja vu all over again when I look at this data. You know, we invest a lot of money, we have a lot of personnel, and let's see, opium cultivation increased by 36 percent between 2012 and 2013 to a record 516,000 acres in Afghanistan, a country where we have troops, we've been fighting a war, difficult but we have a lot more control than if we're not there. And it just—I'm going to be real interested in hearing about progress and what we mean by progress, because what I see is the United States, frankly, losing this war. I don't want it to lose the war, but I'm skeptical about the progress, the milestones being alleged, so I look forward to hearing the testimony of our witnesses. Thank you, Madam Chairman.

Ms. ROS-LEHTINEN. Thank you, Mr. Connolly. And we thank the witnesses for their wonderful patience waiting an hour to start our hearing. But I always say as a Cuban refugee who lost her homeland to communism, I love getting interrupted by votes. This is not a problem.

And first we welcome a dear friend to our subcommittee and to me personally, Ambassador William Brownfield, Assistant Secretary at the State Department's Bureau of International Narcotics and Law Enforcement Affairs.

Prior to his appointment, Ambassador Brownfield was U.S. Ambassador to Colombia, to Venezuela, and to Chile, and has served as Deputy Assistant Secretary for Western Hemisphere Affairs. He holds the personal rank of Career Ambassador, the highest rank in the U.S. Foreign Service. Welcome again, Mr. Ambassador. I think both of us would agree that we would enjoy spending today in a field hearing in Miami instead of being in DC, but welcome.

And next we're so pleased to welcome a gentleman who also has a Miami connection. It's just a coincidence, honestly. We welcome Mr. James Capra who is Chief of Operations at the Drug Enforcement Administration.

Mr. Capra has had a long and distinguished career in law enforcement having served in numerous roles in DEA including a Special Agent in Charge of the Dallas Field Division, and before this as Associate Special Agent in Charge of the Miami Field Division. Prior to his career in law enforcement, Mr. Capra served in the United States Navy, the Navy Reserves, the Air National Guard, and as a military intelligence officer with the U.S. Army Reserves. Thank you, sir, for being with us.

And third, I'm so pleased to welcome to our subcommittee hearing Ms. Erin Logan, Principal Director for Counternarcotics and Global Threats for the Deputy Assistant Secretary of Defense. She previously served as the Chief of Staff and Special Assistant for the Assistant Secretary of Defense in the Office of the Under Secretary of Defense for Policy. Prior to this, she was a senior professional staff member of the Senate Foreign Relations Committee where she was a primary advisor to then-Senator Joe Biden on defense issues. I believe that we has someone here on the dias who has some kind of connection to the Senate Foreign Relations Committee. I'm not sure who it is, Mr. Connolly, but we welcome all three of you to our subcommittee. And, Ambassador Brownfield, we will begin with you, amigo.

### STATEMENT OF THE HONORABLE WILLIAM R. BROWNFIELD, ASSISTANT SECRETARY OF STATE, BUREAU OF INTERNATIONAL NARCOTICS AND LAW ENFORCEMENT AFFAIRS, U.S. DEPARTMENT OF STATE

Ambassador BROWNFIELD. Thank you, Madam Chairman, Ranking Member Deutch, members of the committee. Thank you for the opportunity to appear today to discuss counternarcotics efforts in Afghanistan. I agree with you, Madam Chairman, far better were we having this meeting today in Miami, but we will meet where we are and deal with the world as it is, not as we might wish it would be.

Ladies and gentlemen, I have just returned from Afghanistan last week and I look forward to sharing my observations on this essential topic.

Members of the committee, we know that Afghanistan is the source of more than 80 percent of the world's illegal opiates, and that drugs represent the largest domestic source of income for the Taliban, but there are key facts that we do not know. We do not know the security picture we will encounter after 2014, or the exact contours of the bilateral relationship, or the resources that will be available to us, or the posture of the international community.

We have learned lessons in the past 40 years about anti-drug programs. We learned that drug strategies take time. It takes years to get into a crisis, and years to resolve it. The strategy must be comprehensive. You cannot solve a crisis by addressing just one element. And the strategy must be adaptable, capable of responding to inevitable changes by the trafficking adversary.

Last week in Kabul I discussed INL assistant efforts with the Minister of Counternarcotics and the Minister of Interior. We agreed on the need for a multifaceted approach with strong Afghan Government leadership. We concluded that our drug cooperation should be driven by five guiding principles. First, focus on sustainable Afghan capabilities. Capacity building is more important than equipment, and must be sustainable over the long term. Second, emphasize Afghan priorities and strategies. If there is no Afghan buy-in our strategies will not succeed. Third, deliver on previous commitments. If we lose the trust of the Afghan people cooperation withers. Fourth, integrate international donors and regional partners into the strategy. We cannot do this alone, and they consume far more of the Afghan product than we do. And fifth, given changing security and resource realities after 2014, we must adapt our monitoring and evaluation strategies to continue to insure taxpayer funds are protected and our programs are as effective as they can be.

Members of the committee, you will in my written statement a summary of our counter drug programs in Afghanistan. You will read of programs designed to address crop control, eradication, alternative development, interdiction, prosecution, training and capacity building, and demand reduction. You will read of some of our efforts to engage important international partners in the United Nations, the UK, other European institutions, and Central Asian governments. You will read of our proposed tiered approach to monitoring and evaluation where we use the best available sources to evaluate our programs in the field in light of security and resources. I hope you find a comprehensive and sustainable drug strategy.

Madam Chairman, I detect pessimism in some media reporting on Afghan drugs. I do not share it any more than I shared the pessimism of those who still reported in 2007 that Plan Colombia was a failure. Counternarcotics is critical to the success of Afghanistan post-2014, and requires continued support and attention. I do not promise you success this year or next year, but I do promise with your support a sustainable and adaptable counternarcotics strategy that builds capacities for the Afghan Government to address drug challenges post-2014.

I thank you and I look forward to your questions.

[The prepared statement of Ambassador Brownfield follows:]

UNITED STATES DEPARTMENT OF STATE
BUREAU OF INTERNATIONAL NARCOTICS
AND LAW ENFORCEMENT AFFAIRS


Prepared Statement of:

**Ambassador William R. Brownfield**
Assistant Secretary of State for
International Narcotics & Law Enforcement Affairs


Hearing Before the:

**House Foreign Affairs Committee,
Sub-committee on the Middle East and North Africa**


**"U.S. Counternarcotics Operations in Afghanistan"**


*Wednesday, February 5, 2014*

Chairman Ros-Lehtinen, Ranking Member Deutch, and other distinguished Representatives, thank you for the opportunity to appear before you today to discuss counternarcotics efforts in Afghanistan. The State Department's Bureau of International Narcotics and Law Enforcement Affairs (INL), which I have the honor to lead, works alongside our Afghan partners to help them develop and sustain programs to minimize all stages of the drug trade, including cultivation, production, trafficking, and use; to better protect vulnerable populations from the scourge of drugs; and to bring to justice major traffickers. These programs are works in progress. There is no silver bullet to eliminate drug cultivation or production in Afghanistan or address the epidemic of substance abuse disorders that plagues too many Afghans. But we are successfully building Afghan capacity to implement and lead counternarcotics efforts.

Afghanistan today produces well over 80 percent of the world's illicit opium, undermining good governance and public health, subverting the legal economy, fueling corruption and insecurity, and putting money in the hands of the Taliban. The narcotics trade has been a windfall for the insurgency. The United Nations (UN) estimates that the Afghan Taliban receives at least $155 million annually from narcotics-related activities including taxation, protection, and extortion.

According to the UN World Drug Report, Afghan opium fuels a global trade in heroin that generates over $60 billion total in profits for corrupt officials, drug traffickers, organized criminal groups, and insurgents. And while the Drug Enforcement Administration (DEA) estimates that only a small portion of the heroin in the United States currently originates in Afghanistan, there is clear potential for transnational criminal networks to adapt and for this amount to increase in the years ahead.

Afghan poppy cultivation increased significantly in 2013. While cultivation is only one indicator of counternarcotics progress, it was disappointing news, as was the reported decline in poppy eradication by provincial authorities. With the vast majority of opium poppy cultivated in the least secure areas, poppy farming is inextricably linked to security. Illicit actors, including insurgents, profit from narcotic sales. And in 2014, preparations for the critical spring elections will create competing demands on Afghan security forces who assumed the security lead from international forces only six months ago and continue to build their capacities.

Equally worrisome is the impact of the narcotics trade on Afghanistan's democratic institutions and human development, which the United States has supported through heavy investment. At every level of the illicit narcotics market – from cultivation to production to trafficking and consumption – the narcotics trade undermines good governance and saps the capacity of the Afghan people. It is noteworthy that Afghanistan now has one of the highest opiate usage rates in the world.

Despite these tough realities, we have seen encouraging progress in the Afghan government's counternarcotics capacity. In particular, there have been positive developments in areas such as prosecutions, interdiction, alternative livelihoods for Afghan farmers, and treatment services for substance use disorders. We have also seen that in communities where the government has established a strong foothold and where basic development facilities, such as medical clinics and schools, are available, farmers are less likely to grow poppy.

The Counter Narcotics Justice Center (CNJC), a fully Afghan facility with jurisdiction for the investigation, detention, prosecution, and trial of major narcotics cases is another source of optimism. INL, in partnership with the U.S. Department of Justice and the United Kingdom, provides advisory and facility operations assistance to the CNJC. During the most recent Afghan calendar year (from March 2012 to March 2013), the CNJC's Primary and Appellate Courts each heard the cases of over 700 accused. The CNJC Investigation and Laboratory Department processed cases involving more than 233 metric tons of illegal drugs – a 26 percent increase over the previous year. The CNJC is often cited as one of the premier judicial institutions in Afghanistan and is where U.S.-designated drug kingpin Haji Lal Jan was tried last year and ultimately received a 15-year prison sentence. While in Afghanistan last week, Director Kohistani of the General Directorate of Prisons and Detention Centers and I cut the ribbon on a new INL-funded detention center at the CNJC, enabling a much-needed five-fold expansion in its capacity.

Together with the United Kingdom we have helped the Afghan government stand up skilled Afghan interdiction units with specialized intelligence capabilities. Over the past several years, we have seen a steady increase in the amount of illicit narcotics seized by the Counter Narcotics Police of Afghanistan (CNPA) and its specialized units, which have been trained through U.S. programs. The growing and self-sustaining capacity of these vetted units is the direct result of U.S. mentoring, training, and assistance, which INL implements with our partners at DEA and the Department of Defense. INL successfully transitioned the Kunduz Regional Law Enforcement Center to the Afghan Ministry of the Interior (MOI) in September of 2013. The MOI now manages this center and it continues to be used by CNPA vetted units for sensitive interdiction missions.

Supporting economic alternatives to poppy cultivation is also critical. While alternative development programs are best addressed by my colleagues at the U.S. Agency for International Development, last week Afghan Minister of Counter Narcotics Rashedi and I committed to redesign our signature Good Performers Initiative (GPI) program to further improve its efficacy and ensure that we encourage and reward counternarcotics efforts on all fronts, not just reductions in cultivation. GPI provides development assistance to Afghan provinces that demonstrate significant counternarcotics achievements. Since 2007, this effort has been led by the Afghan Ministry of Counter Narcotics, which plans, implements, and monitors the program, with support and oversight from the United States.

Drug treatment is another area where the Afghan government and civil society are making significant progress. The U.S. and other donors have provided substantial support to enable the Afghans to establish a network of over 100 facilities across the country offering evidence-based treatment services. We are now in the process of transitioning responsibility for all drug treatment services to the Government of Afghanistan. As a first step, the Ministry of Public Health has committed to hiring the clinical staff at all drug treatment centers as government employees, which is critical to ensuring that these programs will be sustained under Afghan ownership in the years ahead.

Our work with the Afghan Ministry of Counter Narcotics (MCN) cuts across all of these efforts. In recent years, the leadership and staff of the MCN have demonstrated increased effectiveness in designing counternarcotics policies across the relevant Afghan ministries and in implementing counternarcotics programs nationwide.

Each of these positive developments has matured in spite of a difficult security environment, entrenched corruption, and criminal groups that have worked to undermine progress. But while the challenges are many, let us also keep them in perspective. Today, poppy is grown on less than three percent of Afghanistan's farmable land – roughly the same amount of land devoted to rice and one tenth as much as is devoted to wheat production. The estimated value of opium to the Afghan economy has remained relatively stable over the last decade. Yet Afghanistan's legal economy has grown steadily. As a result, the potential net export value of opiates now make up a much smaller fraction of Afghanistan's economy. In short, Afghanistan's drug challenge may be formidable, but it is not insurmountable.

As our government's policy makers define the scope and shape of our engagement in Afghanistan post-2014, we will be ready to tailor our security assistance programs accordingly. We are reviewing our INL counternarcotics programs to assess how to enhance their impact and to ensure we can maintain robust oversight even with anticipated reductions in staff mobility. Several principles will guide our efforts:

It will be essential that we help our Afghan partners preserve the capacities they have developed with our support. The Afghan government that emerges from this year's elections will need to possess the capabilities – and the political will – to make further counternarcotics progress in the post-2014 period.

Counternarcotics efforts within Afghanistan are fundamentally the responsibility of the Afghan government and people. This is why, across the board, we will focus even more intensively on building the Afghan government's capacity to successfully and sustainably take responsibility for future efforts.

The Afghan opiate trade extends, however, far beyond Afghanistan. For this reason, we also stress and encourage bilateral and multilateral assistance from the international community, as agreed to in the Tokyo Mutual Accountability Framework, to support counternarcotics efforts in Afghanistan. A number of our partners, including the United Kingdom, Canada, and Japan, already provide significant assistance to build the Afghan government's capacity. We are re-doubling our efforts to bring additional countries to the table, particularly those which are most affected by Afghan opiates. For example, , we recently joined key regional countries – including Afghanistan, Pakistan, India, and China – to address precursor chemicals by identifying best practices, tools for tracking chemicals, and next steps to combat illicit trafficking of precursors.

Our counternarcotics efforts do not take place in a vacuum – they are an integral part of the broader U.S. strategy for Afghanistan. As the U.S. footprint shrinks, we are regularly reviewing our multilayered oversight approach, which includes U.S. direct hires having eyes-on wherever possible, supplemented by locally employed staff, independent third party audits, and reporting from implementing program partners and intergovernmental organizations. Regardless of the shape or scope of our future counternarcotics efforts in Afghanistan, rigorous monitoring, evaluation, and oversight are necessary to ensure that our assistance has a positive and significant impact and that our programs are safeguarded from waste and abuse.

Our experience elsewhere in the world demonstrates that counternarcotics is a long-term effort, hand in glove with the equally long-term challenges of good governance and sustainable economic growth. As we look to the end of 2014, Afghan capacity to weaken narcotics production and trafficking will only become more important. To be successful, Afghan political will is critically important, but we must also sustain assistance with programmatic support and advice. Success generally requires sustained, long term efforts, so that our partners can develop the necessary capabilities to deliver real results. A diverse, well-coordinated set of programs to support Afghan counternarcotics capacity, with support from across the interagency and our partners here on the Hill, will be necessary.

Thank you Chairman Ros-Lehtinen, Ranking Member Deutch, and members of the Sub-committee, for your time. I will do my best to address your questions.

Ms. Ros-Lehtinen. Thank you, Mr. Ambassador. Mr. Capra.

## STATEMENT OF MR. JAMES L. CAPRA, CHIEF OF OPERATIONS, DRUG ENFORCEMENT ADMINISTRATION, U.S. DEPARTMENT OF JUSTICE

Mr. Capra. Chairman Ros-Lehtinen, Ranking Member Deutch and distinguished members of the subcommittee, on behalf of Administrator Leonhart and the Drug Enforcement Administration, I appreciate your invitation to testify today regarding DEA's counternarcotics strategy in Afghanistan.

Madam Chairman, I ask that my written statement be included in the record.

Ms. Ros-Lehtinen. Without objection.

Mr. Capra. Before I get started I would like to thank you, Madam Chairman and Representative Kennedy, for visiting the DEA compound during your last trip. I'd also like to take this opportunity to extend the invitation to any interested committee members for a similar visit.

DEA focuses international efforts on identifying and combating drug trafficking organizations that pose the greatest threat to U.S. interests. We accomplish this by analyzing illicit drug cultivation, manufacturing and transporting trends, transportation trends, tracking the flow of illicit proceeds and money laundering patterns, assessing the law enforcement capabilities and potential growth of our foreign counterparts, providing mentorship, training, and other assistance to help those counterparts build capacity and achieve strategic and tactical effectiveness, supporting programs promoting the Rule of Law worldwide and unifying and harmonizing efforts to bring to justice transnational drug traffickers and narcoterrorists.

The United Nations has estimated that the international drug trade generates $322 billion per year in revenue, making drugs by far the most lucrative illicit activity. According to the U.N., revenues from other types of transnational criminal activities such as arms trafficking and alien smuggling are small by comparison.

The narcotics trade in Afghanistan undermines the economic development, enables corruption, erodes government legitimacy, facilitates transnational organized crime, and threatens stability and security in the Rule of Law in Afghanistan and across the region.

The Taliban receives millions annually from the narcotics-related activities. With poppy cultivation increasing in the country, it can be assumed Taliban profits will also continue to rise fueling further instability worldwide.

DEA is fully supportive of the Government of Afghanistan and its national drug control strategy. This strategy reaffirms U.S. commitment to breaking the narcotics insurgency nexus in Afghanistan and reinforcing the legitimacy of governmental institution. With the expected drawdown of U.S. combat forces, DEA efforts will remain focused on supporting counternarcotics programs which are both effective and sustainable. We understand these challenges. With the assistance of our interagency colleagues we stand ready to tackle the mission.

DEA will transition our role in Afghanistan to correspond with traditional DEA overseas operations. We will continue to collect drug-related intelligence supporting domestic DEA investigations, as well as joint investigation with our host nation counterparts. To meet this commitment, DEA must maintain a sufficient staffing level in Afghanistan.

DEA continues to develop the capability and capacity of the special vetted units of the counternarcotics police in Afghanistan to address the illicit drug trade. Our Afghan partners are already conducting independent investigations and trying and convicting drug traffickers in Afghan courts.

The threat from the drug trade in Afghanistan is far from over. It is critical that we sustain the positive momentum to preserve security gains made over the past decade.

Administrator Leonhart and the men and women of the DEA are committed to standing with our interagency colleagues and Afghan counterparts to build a sustainable and effective counternarcotics program in Afghanistan that protects U.S. national security interests.

Madam Chair, I thank you for your time and look forward to your questions.

[The prepared statement of Mr. Capra follows:]

# Department of Justice

STATEMENT OF

**JAMES L. CAPRA**
**CHIEF OF OPERATIONS**
**DRUG ENFORCEMENT ADMINISTRATION**
**U.S. DEPARTMENT OF JUSTICE**

BEFORE THE

**COMMITTEE ON FOREIGN AFFAIRS**
**SUBCOMMITTEE ON THE MIDDLE EAST AND NORTH AFRICA**
**U.S. HOUSE OF REPRESENTATIVES**

FOR A HEARING ENTITLED

**"FUTURE U.S. COUNTERNARCOTICS EFFORTS IN AFGHANISTAN"**

PRESENTED ON

**FEBRUARY 5, 2014**

**Statement of James L. Capra**
**Chief of Operations, Drug Enforcement Administration**
**Before the House Committee on Foreign Affairs,**
**Subcommittee on the Middle East and North Africa**
**"Future U.S. Counternarcotics Efforts in Afghanistan"**
**February 5, 2014**

Chairman Ros-Lehtinen, Ranking Member Deutch, and distinguished members of Subcommittee, on behalf of Administrator Leonhart and the Drug Enforcement Administration (DEA), I appreciate your invitation to testify today regarding DEA's counternarcotics (CN) strategy in Afghanistan.

Introduction

The July 2010 *U.S. Counternarcotics Strategy in Afghanistan* report by the Senate Caucus on International Narcotics Control stated that, "United States Policy makers need to recognize that the Taliban operates as a drug cartel and that the drug trade in Afghanistan must be addressed with the same level of resolve as the insurgency – by utilizing every means available." The Caucus concluded that "[i]f the U.S. Government ignores the drug problem, we will fail in Afghanistan."

DEA's core mission is to disrupt and dismantle the most significant drug trafficking organizations posing the greatest threat to the United States. The DEA program in Afghanistan is designed to deny narcotics-generated funding to terrorism and the insurgency, break the nexus between the insurgency and drug trafficking, promote the rule of law, and expose and reduce corruption, while diminishing the overall drug threat from Afghanistan.

Background

Afghanistan, as the world's largest source of illicit opium, figures predominantly in the U.S. long-term strategy to address drug trafficking. Opium, morphine base, heroin, and hashish produced in Afghanistan are trafficked world-wide. DEA, in its unique capacity as the world's preeminent drug law enforcement agency, identifies, investigates, disrupts, and targets individuals and drug trafficking organizations (DTOs) responsible for the production and distribution of illegal drugs. DEA is responsible for enforcing the provisions of domestic controlled substances and chemical diversion trafficking laws, and consequently serves as the nation's primary agency for ensuring national compliance with the provisions of international drug control treaties. To accomplish this, it is essential that DEA share its knowledge and expertise with our foreign counterparts, as well as develop strong working relationships with them.

Although Afghanistan produces an estimated 80 percent of the world's illicit opiates, currently only limited quantities of heroin found in American cities is of Afghan origin. The primary markets for Southwest Asian opiates continue to be Europe, Russia, Iran, Central Asia, Southeast Asia, China and, increasingly, coastal Africa. The nexus between drug trafficking and the insurgency in Afghanistan continues to grow and is not a new trend. Insurgent groups in Afghanistan utilize drug trafficking proceeds to advance their political agendas. Terrorist groups utilize alternative sources of financing, including fundraising from sympathizers, including certain nongovernmental organizations, and criminal activities such as arms trafficking, money laundering, kidnap-for-ransom, extortion, racketeering, and drug trafficking. Terrorist groups often seek to exploit these economic activities in their areas of influence; this is particularly true with drug trafficking due to its lucrative nature and international prevalence. The Taliban is involved in taxing opium poppy farmers; operating processing laboratories; moving narcotics; taxing narcotics transported through Taliban checkpoints and/or Taliban controlled territory; providing security to poppy fields, drug labs, and opium bazaars; and collecting "donations."

The Government of Afghanistan developed its National Drug Control Strategy in cooperation with international partners. This strategy reaffirms the U.S. commitment to assist Afghanistan in breaking the narcotics-insurgency nexus and reinforcing the legitimacy of its governmental institutions. Given the drawdown of U.S. combat forces in Afghanistan, DEA's efforts are focused on supporting effective and sustainable Afghan CN programs.

The Situation Today

The narcotics trade in Afghanistan undermines licit economic development, enables corruption, erodes government legitimacy, facilitates other forms of transnational organized crime, and threatens stability, security, and rule of law in Afghanistan and across the region. Sustaining the successful security transition to Afghan forces will rest in part on limiting insurgents' access to drug-related funding and support.

In response to this challenge, in 2003, DEA reopened the Kabul Country Office (CO) in Afghanistan. By the end of fiscal year (FY) 2013, DEA had NSDD-38 approval for a total of 97 authorized positions in Afghanistan. This authorized staffing level includes 82 permanent positions plus 15 temporary duty positions (TDY). The TDY positions include 3 pilots and 12 Foreign-deployed Advisory and Support Team (FAST) members. Additionally, the DEA Kabul CO is supported by 13 contract employees, including 4 intelligence analysts, 3 pilots, 5 air wing mechanics/avionics technicians, and 1 office network technician. In FY 2014, DEA will gradually reduce staffing in a manner consistent with the U.S. military drawdown and Administration priorities.

DEA's efforts in Afghanistan are supported through both direct annual appropriations and reimbursable agreements with the Departments of State (DoS) and Defense (DoD). In FY 2013, DEA dedicated approximately $17 million of its annual appropriation to provide all necessary support for 13 permanent positions, plus the FAST personnel and TDY pilots in Afghanistan.

In FY 2013, DEA also received $30.5 million from the DoS Bureau of South and Central Asia Affairs (DoS-SCA) primarily for personnel-related costs; and $6.6 million from DoD for the operation and maintenance of aircraft, $8.7 million for the startup costs associated with Global Discovery Aircraft, and $350,000 for staffing reimbursements. DEA also received $16.2 million for program costs from the DoS Bureau of International Narcotics and Law Enforcement Affairs (DoS-INL), available for use between FY 2012-2014, and to date, DoS-SCA has committed

$15.9 million for personnel and program costs in FY 2014. DEA and DoS-SCA are still working to determine the remaining resource requirements for FY 2014.

## Vetted Units and Capacity-Building

The Kabul CO is engaged in a decade- long effort to assist the Afghan government by developing Ministry of Interior specialized units of the Counternarcotics Police-Afghanistan (CNP-A) and working to break the country's nexus between narcotics and public corruption. DEA, with support from DoD and DoS, has developed the CNP-A, through training and mentoring, to be able – on its own – to investigate, arrest, and assist in the prosecution of high level drug traffickers. The DEA is actively involved in, and remains committed to, continuing to mature the CNP-A.

DEA was also instrumental in standing up the Afghan National Interdiction Unit (NIU), the Sensitive Investigative Unit (SIU), and the Technical Investigative Unit (TIU), a sub-unit of the SIU. The DEA Office of Training, in conjunction with the U.S. Central Command and Kabul CO, has also provided oversight for the Afghanistan Regional Training Team (RTT). The RTT provides basic, sustainment and advanced training to members of the CNP-A and its specialized enforcement units, the NIU, the SIU, and the TIU. For each of these three units, DEA has provided guidance to the Afghans on developing, conducting and taking an active leadership role in investigations and operations, as well as provided advice on building a sustainable organizational structure and resolving inter-agency issues.

DEA continues to develop the capability and capacity of the specialized vetted units of the CNP-A to address the illicit drug trade. Enabling the vetted units of the CNP-A to independently combat the narcotics trade, with gradually increasing degrees of responsibility and ownership, will reinforce broader U.S. security goals in the region. Candidates for the Afghanistan vetted units are carefully chosen from within the CNP-A based on professional, psychological, physical, and stringent ethical standards. All vetted unit members to include the NIU, SIU and TIU undergo background checks, urinalysis, and Leahy Vetting to ensure the most trustworthy personnel are selected for the program. SIU candidates are held to an even higher standard and are subjected to polygraph examinations conducted by DEA and receive training at the DEA Academy in Quantico, Virginia. In addition to this initial vetting process, members are randomly selected for polygraph exams and urinalysis testing during their assignment to the SIU.

DEA's capacity-building efforts include: training, providing equipment and infrastructure, and mentoring by DEA enforcement, intelligence, and training personnel. The vetted units (NIU, SIU and TIU) require specialized equipment and mentoring in technical investigative techniques, namely wire intercept equipment and in the investigative analysis of information obtained from these intercepts. DEA has provided operation and maintenance support for the Judicial Wire Intercept Program (JWIP) system as well as contract intelligence analysts to mentor Afghan law enforcement officers in the proper investigative techniques for analyzing intercepted conversations.

The NIU is a professional cadre of law enforcement personnel specially trained and equipped to safely make arrests and serve search warrants, and actively supports the SIU with a full range of capabilities, from providing security for undercover officers meeting with drug traffickers, to air mobile operations targeting clandestine drug labs and storage sites. All investigative efforts and enforcement operations are conducted under Afghan law, which enhances the legitimacy of the Afghan government.

The RTT was formed to assist in building capacity and professionalism within Afghanistan's CN security forces. The prime focus for the RTT is to train the DEA mentored vetted units within the CNP-A. The training provided by the RTT plays an integral role in efforts to target the most significant drug trafficking networks, collect evidence, and arrest and prosecute drug traffickers in accordance with Afghan law. The RTT programs provide Afghan trainees with mentoring, training, and direct operational support, with the objective of making the CNP-A, NIU, and SIU capable of independent operations. In 2013, the RTT taught over 500 classes with approximately 10,000 Afghan students.

During the past nine months, the CNP-A initiated and led 2,490 operations in distinct parts of the country. As a result, 2,258 arrests were made, 55 drug labs were destroyed, over 60,619 liters and 32,214 kg of chemicals and over 121 metric tons of drugs were seized. The defendants arrested in these investigations are being prosecuted through the Afghan judicial system.

Financial Threat

The United Nations (UN) has estimated that the international drug trade generates $322 billion per year in revenue, making drugs by far the most lucrative illicit activity. According to the UN, revenues from other types of illicit transnational activity, such as arms trafficking and alien smuggling, are small by comparison. Drugs provide many different avenues of revenue, including the taxing of farmers and local cartels, and the provision of security for all aspects of production, trade, and distribution. Terror organizations do not, in general, require massive sums of money for their operations, but must finance training, infrastructure needs, equipping their members, bribing local officials, recruiting, and logistics. Major criminal patronage networks are targeted for investigation and prosecution, especially those supporting terrorism and the insurgency. DEA's SIU program, which is used in a dozen countries, has proven to be highly successful in Afghanistan. Within the Afghan SIU, DEA established the SIU-Financial Investigation Team (SIU-FIT), a sub-unit of financial investigators mentored by the DEA-led Afghanistan Threat Finance Cell (ATFC); which is co-led by DoD and includes a detailee from the Department of the Treasury.

The ATFC utilized its multi-agency law enforcement personnel and its close working relationship with the vetted Afghan SIU-FIT and the Central Bank's Financial Transactions and Reports Analysis Center for Afghanistan (FINTRACA), to become a major hub for terrorist and illicit finance intelligence collection, analysis and dissemination. Information from ATFC is available to the law enforcement, intelligence, military and diplomatic communities. The threat finance networks in Afghanistan consist of mutually-beneficial relationships between the insurgency, narcotics traffickers, unscrupulous members of the financial and commercial sectors, and corrupt public officials. These relationships create the networks that the ATFC targets. This has led the ATFC to build target packages and provide information for designations pursuant to the counterterrorism authority of E.O. 13224 and the Foreign Narcotics Kingpin Designation Act. It also develops high-level corruption investigations with the SIU-FIT.

The ATFC, in conjunction with Afghan authorities, has developed a list of core competencies for Afghan financial investigators and a robust training program for the SIU-FIT that are expected to develop of a cadre of Afghan financial investigators who can work independently of foreign mentorship. In fact, the SIU-FIT is already conducting investigations without ATFC involvement, but with ATFC leadership – at the Afghans' request – periodically reviewing the work.

During the last two years alone, the DEA-supervised ATFC law enforcement element has identified and disrupted multiple terrorist networks, including the Herat Insurgent Network, which was led by Abdullah AKBARI. AKBARI's network has murdered over 100 Afghan civilians and smuggled weapons, drugs, and money for Al Qaeda, the Taliban, and other Islamic extremist groups. AKBARI was killed during an arrest attempt.

In addition, DEA, in coordination with DoD, continues to implement the Afghan JWIP, the installation of which was approved by President Karzai, that provides admissible evidence for use in courts of law in Afghanistan, the United States, and other nations. The JWIP is staffed by the CNP-A TIU, by officers selected from the SIU based on their technical aptitude for working wire intercepts and conducting analysis. Additionally, vetted civilian translators work with the TIU and provide monitoring and linguistic support. This judicial intercept program, reviewed by prosecutors and authorized by judges, is used by the SIU to develop prosecutable cases against DTOs operating in and around Afghanistan. Since its inception in December 2008, JWIP efforts have led to several successful prosecutions in Afghanistan.

### Foreign-deployed Advisory Support Teams (FAST)

One of five, 10-member FAST teams trained by U.S. Special Forces rotate to Afghanistan every 120 days. This allows for interoperability with U.S. Special Forces and the North Atlantic Treaty Organizations' International Security Assistance Force. FAST augments the agency's workforce and capabilities in Afghanistan and partners with the NIU to identify, target, disrupt, and dismantle DTOs.

### Special Operations Division (SOD)

DEA's SOD operations directly support Afghan law enforcement activities, including SIU and TIU efforts directed against significant drug trafficking organizations. While coordinating cases with SOD, Afghan vetted units learn the investigative techniques required to identify, investigate, and take down extensive drug trafficking organizations. The long-term development, establishment, and maintenance of high-level confidential sources (CS), is one of the primary objectives of SOD's enforcement groups. The Kabul CO and their Afghan partners in the vetted units work together to identify, recruit, and direct these CSs. These CSs are then used proactively to target the most significant drug traffickers, money launderers, terrorists, and narcoterrorists in the region.

SOD also directs regional investigations with the goal of indictment, extradition of fugitives to the United States, and prosecution in the United States utilizing statutes with extra-territorial jurisdiction. SOD has assigned a Special Agent to the Kabul CO from its Counter-Narcoterrorism Operations Center (CNTOC) that provides operational coordination with the intelligence community on all of DEA's narcoterrorism related investigations.

CNTOC's assigned personnel provide direct support to the Kabul CO and its Afghan counterparts on its investigations and coordinate the investigations with Afghanistan's neighboring countries. This close coordination and real time response to Kabul CO investigations allows the office to have the greatest possible impact on complex investigations of international DTOs.

Aviation Support

DEA's Aviation program permits the successful pursuit of drug investigations and other DEA mission objectives in an otherwise hostile environment. The program's flexibility and ability to minimize operational delays and barriers is unique for civilian programs in the region.

Interagency Operations Coordination Center (IOCC)

The IOCC's mission is to provide CN network analysis and targeting support to U.S. and United Kingdom (UK)-mentored Afghan agencies and to de-conflict CN targets and operations, as well as support law enforcement agencies. Its objectives are to assist the CNP-A to arrest and present for prosecution significant traffickers and key associates to the Afghan judicial system. The IOCC is led by a director and deputy director; those positions rotate annually between senior managers of DEA and the UK's National Crime Agency, formerly the Serious Organized Crime Agency. The two primary action arms that the IOCC supports are the DEA-mentored NIU and the UK-mentored Afghan National Security Force.

Challenges ahead

DEA currently relies heavily on the U.S. military for force protection, airlift and close air support, and in extremis support during the execution of CN operations. The scope of DEA's counterdrug operations will be reduced without U.S. military and coalition forces to support field operations throughout Afghanistan, particularly in uncontrolled areas throughout Helmand and Kandahar.

Currently, the Government of Afghanistan is not capable of absorbing or replicating the scale of assistance provided by the international community, and further attention must be given to developing Afghan policymaking and programmatic capacity to ensure that Afghan law enforcement agencies can successfully operate in a challenging security environment.

In December 2012, DEA and the interagency community developed an updated *U.S. Counternarcotics Strategy for Afghanistan* focused on strengthening the Afghan government's capacity to combat the drug trade, counter the link between narcotics and the insurgency, and disrupt drug-related funding to the insurgency. This strategy prioritizes U.S. CN assistance during the security transition and upcoming drawdown of U.S. combat forces. It establishes the basis for cooperation over the next decade, including shared commitments to combat terrorism and strengthen democratic institutions.

Consistent within this strategic framework, the United States remains committed to helping the Government of Afghanistan break the narcotics-insurgency nexus and further connect its people to their government. The DEA supports a CN plan in Afghanistan that is realistic, durable, sustainable, and that protects U.S. national security interests. Ultimately, Afghan leadership must be capable of providing security and executing CN programs.

Looking Forward

To respond to these challenges, DEA will need to transition its operational profile to more closely correspond with traditional DEA operations overseas – conducting bilateral investigations that target significant trafficking organizations while advising and assisting selected host nation law enforcement units, collecting drug-related intelligence, and supporting domestic DEA investigations. In order to meet this objective, the Kabul CO will focus narrowly on partnering with the SIU and NIU of the CNP-A in order to sustain the level of capacity and capability to conduct significant investigations and to execute effective operations that have been laboriously built over a decade of conflict.

During the security transition and continuing drawdown of U.S. combat forces, DEA will also be drawing down to a level that will represent its new normal staffing level in Afghanistan and DEA will confront a challenging security environment post-2014.

Staffing

The CN capability that the Government of Afghanistan currently demonstrates has been achieved at great cost. It represents years of great sacrifice by DEA personnel and an enormous expenditure of U.S. Government resources. The erosion of this capability puts at risk the U.S. strategic objective of achieving a stable and secure Afghanistan, given the destabilizing effect drug trafficking presents.

DEA plans to maintain a minimum staffing level in Afghanistan post-2014. The Kabul CO will continue to provide support to both the SIU and NIU through training, mentoring and coordination to ensure successful outcomes for the significant bilateral investigations and joint operations conducted by these specialized units.

Given the size and the complexity of the NIU's operational missions, DEA may supplement the Kabul CO advisory effort to the NIU with periodic deployments of FAST personnel. FAST personnel can provide the Kabul CO with mission-specific skills, such as Personnel Recovery of DEA personnel, assisting the Kabul CO and their SIU/NIU counterparts with complex investigation planning and execution of interdiction programs, and managing enforcement operations in a high threat environment with limited resources and support.

## International Coordination

DEA will continue to facilitate the integration of Afghanistan into the broader, regional effort to reduce heroin trafficking. Given the inherent difficulties of fostering effective partnerships among the various participants, DEA is often called upon to facilitate the level of trust required to pursue multilateral investigations.

While much can be accomplished by the partners in the region, more can be accomplished if Afghanistan retains and grows its capacity to be an effective partner. When one considers that virtually all of the heroin trafficked in or through the region is of Afghan origin, the continued success of the NIU and the SIU, to include the JWIP, will provide a wealth of investigative leads to other partner nations.

## Conclusion

DEA's enduring presence in Afghanistan is designed to preserve security gains made over the past decade and to disrupt and dismantle the most significant DTOs posing the greatest threat to the United States. DEA, through a partnership with the Afghans, plans to continue to disrupt DTOs, contain the flow of drugs from Afghanistan, dismantle threat networks, and work with external partners to coordinate CN efforts in the region, but the extent of DEA's efforts post-2014 will be impacted by the mission and footprint of U.S. forces in Afghanistan after 2014.

DEA believes that a reduced staffing presence, plus FAST and TDY pilot support, will allow the continuation of critical CN operations in Afghanistan post-2014. While DEA will be able to sustain much of the advances it has made, especially the build-up of Afghan vetted unit capabilities, the U.S. military drawdown in Afghanistan and corresponding decreases in DEA staffing levels will significantly impact the scope of DEA's operations.

Thank you for the opportunity to testify before the Subcommittee today, and we look forward to working together with you on CN Operations in Afghanistan.

Ms. ROS-LEHTINEN. Thank you, sir. Ms. Logan, thank you very much.

## STATEMENT OF MS. ERIN LOGAN, PRINCIPAL DIRECTOR FOR COUNTERNARCOTICS AND GLOBAL THREATS, OFFICE OF THE UNDER SECRETARY OF DEFENSE, U.S. DEPARTMENT OF DEFENSE

Ms. LOGAN. Thank you, Madam Chair, Ranking Member Deutch, and other members of the subcommittee for the opportunity to talk to you today about the Defense Department's counternarcotics or CN work in Afghanistan and our plans post-2014.

As the members of the subcommittee know well, since 2001 the United States has made an extraordinary investment in blood and Treasury to eliminate the terrorist safe haven that Afghanistan had become. To date, 2,303 Americans have lost their lives in Operation Enduring Freedom, another 19,639 have been wounded. DoD has invested approximately $2 billion in dedicated CN training and programs which is a small fraction of the over $570 billion the nation has spent on the war since 2001.

That said, we do believe that $2 billion has been well spent. We have CN seed, if you will, that has now sprouted and it includes all of the elements that we believe we need to successfully grow, but that growth will only happen if we nurture and protect that which we have planted.

As we look at the future for Afghanistan, it is impossible to envision success without sustaining an Afghan capability to fight the violence and corruption created by the drug trade. In addition, we cannot ignore the growing threat to ourselves and our allies. Our Canadian partners estimate that 90 percent of the heroin on their streets comes from Afghanistan. They also believe they are seeing more heroin than their user population can absorb.

We must all be sensitive to information like this when combined with the Governor of Vermont issuing a State of the State speech focused entirely on Vermont's exploding heroin and opiate problem. We have to realize and be vigilant there is a possibility that Afghan produced heroin will become more available across the United States. DoD as always is committed to disrupting the flow of these drugs as far away from our shores as possible.

Our CN strategy for post-2014 can be summarized by saying that we believe we must focus in three key areas, continued support for vetted units, continued aviation capacity building, and the continued leveraging of our international and interagency capabilities.

First, the vetted units. These units have shown that they are willing and able to do the job, and more and more vetted units are now able to plan, execute, and follow through on CN missions on their own. For example, in December, on December 18th, the DoD supported, DEA mentored Sensitive Investigative Unit was able to use judicial wire taps to build a case that led to the arrest of two criminals, the seizure of 660 grams of heroin, 500 boxes of ammunition, 40 remote controlled IEDs, and 75 rocket propelled grenades. This is a great example of using CN capability to disrupt and remove lethal threats from the battlefield.

Second, our continued support for aviation capacity building. I cannot overstate how vital we believe this is for the terrain of Afghanistan. For any security effort and certainly to run effective CN operations we must enhance the effectiveness and safety of the aviation unit. My office's focus has been the Special Mission Wing which has demonstrated the capability to completely plan and execute operations without international assistance. The Special Mission Wing is just now starting to get the aircraft they need to simultaneously run operations, continue training personnel, and conduct more intensive aircraft maintenance training.

As has been mentioned by my colleagues, our experience in Colombia and elsewhere illustrates that it can take more than a decade for aviation capability to become self-sustaining. In a nation like Afghanistan, the pressures will be very high and it may take longer, but with sustained support we are confident the Special Mission Wing can continue to progress.

Third, I would be remiss if I don't point out that the vetted units and aviation capability are part of a complete structure that the interagency and international community have worked hard to create. You'll see in my written testimony a lot of examples, but one thing that I'd like to highlight is that we believe the drawdown in Afghanistan demands that we explore creative ways to retain some of the effective targeting and intelligence fusion that we've been able to develop with our international interagency partners. Starting small, we believe we can support a regional hub for those capabilities by modestly expanding our current work done by law enforcement intelligence to facilitate interdictions, seizures, investigations, and prosecution. This would be done by slowly expanding the successful but small Operation Riptide already in Bahrain.

Our vision is to create a reach back capability for Afghanistan and a more effective capability for targeting the illicit traffic that is departing the Mokran coast of Pakistan and Iran to go to Africa and beyond.

One great example our Canadian partners have is the HMCS Toronto had seven seizures in 2013. We estimate at DoD that 1 percent of the value of what they removed from the high seas is equal to the amount of funding necessary to outfit a platoon of insurgents.

A regional targeting center would allow us to retain these valuable interagency international partnerships. Again, we believe that the fight against illicit heroin networks in Afghanistan is vital and an important component of insuring that we honor the sacrifice that we have already made. This effort is also necessary to protect vulnerable populations globally, not just from the scourge of addiction, but also from the corruption and violence these networks bring. Our adversaries make good use of these networks to destabilize territory and hurt U.S. interests. We must be equally committed to countering these threats with our networks of creative and capable partners both at home and overseas. I look forward to your questions.

[The prepared statement of Ms. Logan follows:]

**Statement for the Record**
**Erin M. Logan**
**Principal Director for Counternarcotics and Global Threats**
**Office of the Secretary of Defense**

**Before the House Committee on Foreign Affairs**
**Middle East and North Africa Subcommittee**
**"Department of Defense Counternarcotics Efforts in Afghanistan"**
**February 5, 2014**

Chairman Ros-Lehtinen, Representative Deutch, and other distinguished members of the

Subcommittee, thank you for the opportunity to discuss the Department of Defense's (DoD)

counternarcotics, or "CN," efforts in Afghanistan and our strategic vision for CN support in 2014

and beyond. In October, we submitted to Congress DoD's *Post-2014 CN Strategy for Afghanistan*

*and the Region* which outlines our approach to addressing these threats in light of significantly

reduced military force levels inside Afghanistan. Of course, our efforts will ultimately be scoped

and sized by the U.S. government's post-2014 total presence in Afghanistan.

As the Members of this Subcommittee well know, since 2001, the United States has made

an extraordinary investment in blood and treasure to eliminate the terrorist safe haven Afghanistan

had become. To date, over 2,000 Americans have lost their lives in Operation Enduring Freedom

and another nearly 20,000 have been wounded. DoD has invested approximately $2 billion for

dedicated CN training and programs, which is a small fraction of the almost $570 billion we've

spent on the war since 2001 (through FY 2013), and we believe that $2 billion has been well spent

in developing specialized CN units and capabilities that have begun to achieve concrete results.

Despite the progress made in building Afghan CN capabilities, these gains are not yet irreversible

and these nascent institutions will continue to require sustained international support for the

foreseeable future - particularly for resource-intensive programs such as aviation. Like a seedling that has recently sprouted, these organizations have great potential but will require care and nurturing before they are ready to stand on their own. With the upcoming reduction in U.S. and coalition forces and other international capabilities, sustainment will be all the more important. Stepping back from our efforts now would jeopardize the further development of these units that have become reliable partners for U.S. and international law enforcement efforts. I'd like to begin by sharing some observations from the DoD perspective and highlighting a few of the main points I'd like to leave you with.

Afghanistan Drug Threat

As illustrated by resurgent opium production in 2013, the instability caused by the illicit drug trade remains a major obstacle to the long-term security and prosperity of Afghanistan and the region. Recognizing the severity of this threat, the Department invested in counter-drug training and programs during the course of Operation Enduring Freedom to build partner capacity and support U.S. law enforcement and other interagency partners' efforts to weaken drug trafficking networks.

As we look at the future for Afghanistan, it is impossible to envision success without sustaining an Afghan capability to fight the violence and corruption created by the drug trade. Illicit narcotics - although a shrinking proportion of Afghanistan's lawful economy - contributes to insecurity, corruption, poor governance, and stagnation of economic development. Addressing the drug trade and its effects is essential to the successful transition of security responsibility to the Government of Afghanistan. According to the United Nations Office on Drugs and Crime (UNODC), 209,000 hectares of opium poppy were cultivated in 2013, a 36% increase from the 154,000 hectares cultivated in 2012. Additionally, the UNODC estimates that potential opium production in Afghanistan increased from 3,700 metric tons in 2012 to 5,500 metric tons in 2013, which is approximately 49% greater than UNODC's estimate for consumption globally of approximately 3,700 metric tons.

The link between insecurity and opium cultivation is well established in Afghanistan. Most of the opium poppy cultivation is concentrated in southern and western provinces where the narcotics trade continues to fuel criminal and insurgent networks. Insurgents tax local poppy farmers, and in return, provide farmers with loans, material support, and protection for their operations. Insurgents also charge a protection tax to traffickers and labs. The production of opium competes with the country's lawful agriculture industry, distorts other legitimate businesses by undercutting them to launder profits, degrades revenue collection, and undermines public health.

The illicit drug trade originating from Afghan opium extends well beyond the borders of Afghanistan, Central Asia, Iran, and Pakistan's Makran Coast. The trade in Afghan-produced opiates has become an increasingly global phenomenon, with drugs and illicit proceeds flowing to the Persian Gulf and the Middle East, East Africa, Europe, Russia, and North America, with a small percentage of the heroin consumed in the United States coming from Afghanistan. The ripple effect of the heroin trade undermines stability in key regions of U.S. interest, fuels corruption, undermines legitimate economic activity, and provides vital revenue for terrorist groups and other transnational criminal organizations that threaten U.S. security interests worldwide.

In addition, we cannot ignore the growing threat to ourselves and our Allies. For instance, our Canadian partners believe they are seeing more heroin than their user population can absorb.

We must also be sensitive to information such as Vermont Governor Peter Shumlin's "state of the state" speech which focused entirely on Vermont's exploding prescription drug abuse and heroin problem, and Ohio Attorney General Mike DeWine recently declaring heroin an epidemic, with the number of heroin overdoses in Ohio doubling in 2012. While the vast majority of heroin consumed in the United States continues to originate in the Western Hemisphere, we must be vigilant about the possibility of Afghan-produced heroin becoming more available across the United States. DoD, as always, is committed to disrupting the flow of these drugs as far away from our shores as possible.

### DoD CN Efforts in Afghanistan

DoD's CN efforts in Afghanistan support the U.S. government's interagency strategy to counter and disrupt drug-related funding to the insurgency, and second, to strengthen the Afghan government's capacity to combat the drug trade during and after the security transition. Over the past decade, DoD has worked to build the capacity of the Counternarcotics Police of Afghanistan, or CNPA, improve border security, promote information sharing, and foster regional and international cooperation. Despite the increased opium production this past year, DoD-supported efforts have made steady progress building the capacity of specialized Afghan CN units. While, none of these efforts individually can solve this problem, interdiction operations are a key component of a holistic strategy to address all phases of the drug trade and can be successful in reducing insurgent financing from narcotics.

The Departments of Defense, State, Justice (including the Drug Enforcement Administration (DEA)), and Homeland Security, have collaborated to build the law enforcement capacity of

Afghanistan's Ministry of Interior. Information sharing and the ability of Afghan law enforcement and CN forces to prosecute traffickers are integral parts of this infrastructure. The DEA-mentored specialized units within the CNPA continue to demonstrate successful evidence-based operations and serve as key partners in law enforcement efforts. The Afghan Counter-Narcotics Justice Center continues to successfully prosecute narcotics traffickers, including the conviction of Haji Lal Jan Ishaqzai, a U.S. Treasury-designated "kingpin" in 2013, who was convicted and sentenced to 15 years in Afghanistan's prison system.

In partnership with the Department of Justice's (DOJ) International Criminal Investigative Training Assistance Program, DoD established the Counternarcotics Development Unit to coordinate the development of the CNPA in support of ISAF's police development mission. The CNPA continues to make progress and has become a reliable counterdrug law enforcement partner. The Defense Intelligence Agency reports that from January 1, 2013 through December 17, 2013, 2,297 Afghan-led operations resulted in the seizure of 72,433 kilograms (kg) of opium, 11,962 kg of morphine, 6,203 kg of heroin, 31,647 kg of hashish, and 64,784 kg of chemicals.

Effective border management plays a vital role in the future stability and prosperity of the Government of Afghanistan. Customs and other border management agencies help disrupt the flow of illicit narcotics, weapons, and terrorists across international borders; collect taxes and tariffs; protect public health and cultural heritage; and facilitate legitimate trade and travel. DoD also supports the U.S. Embassy Kabul's Border Management Task Force (BMTF) that provides critical training to Afghan customs officials and improved border and customs infrastructure and equipment critical to enhancing their border security capacity. BMTF deploys 65 advisors to critical locations across Afghanistan including the Kabul International Airport. DoD supports the Department of Homeland Security's efforts focusing on mentoring, illicit finance, counter-improvised explosive devices (IEDs), and bulk cash smuggling.

Due to the severe topography and security environment of Afghanistan, aviation support is a key enabler of interdiction operations that deny drug traffickers freedom of action in remote areas. DoD provides CN funding to support the Afghan Special Missions Wing (SMW) which provides aviation support to DEA and Afghan CN law enforcement organizations and special operations forces. This air mobility capability allows Afghan specialized CN units to conduct enforcement efforts with a greater degree of effectiveness and safety, in areas where it would be impractical to infiltrate by other means. With the drawdown of U.S. and coalition forces, we expect that air mobility will continue to be critical to maintaining CN law enforcement effectiveness.

The capabilities of the SMW aircrews have shown impressive development in the last year. As an example, in July 2013, the SMW supported an all-Afghan air and ground force tactical assault interdiction mission. Six Mi-17 helicopters with all-Afghan crews provided tactical insertion and extraction of a 74-man, National Interdiction Unit, all-Afghan ground assault force. The air mission was planned, briefed, and executed without the direct assistance of Coalition Air Advisors and supported a successful CN operation yielding the destruction of 1,500 kg opium, 500 kg hashish, and 25 kg heroin, and the confiscation of 10 AK-47 assault rifles.

DoD CN authorities enable DoD to provide significant analytical support to law enforcement agencies, integrating intelligence and law enforcement information for use in the investigation and prosecution of criminal networks. At the strategic level, DoD supports the Joint

Narcotics Analysis Center (JNAC), a joint U.S./United Kingdom initiative that provides strategic

and operational-level decision-makers with analysis on the narcotics trade in Afghanistan and the

surrounding region. The JNAC provides reach back support for intelligence and law enforcement

organizations in Afghanistan and improved collaboration across a wide spectrum of CN

partnerships. The JNAC is an effective model of interagency and international collaboration and

partnership.

At the operational level, DoD provides support to the law enforcement-led Interagency

Operations Coordination Center (IOCC). The IOCC was established to de-conflict and coordinate

support for law enforcement CN activities in Afghanistan. The IOCC has become an important

source of targeting information and drug trade analysis. At the tactical level, Combined Joint

Interagency Task Force – Nexus (CJIATF-N) was established to provide tactical support to military

and law enforcement organizations to counter narcotics threats and corruption in partnership with

host-nation forces. As U.S. and coalition military forces transition from their combat role, CJIATF-

N will be discontinued and the IOCC will be reduced in size.

The Afghanistan Threat Finance Cell (ATFC) was established in 2008 to identify and

disrupt sources of insurgent and terrorist funding in Afghanistan. This organization is co-led by

DEA and DoD. However, as the 2014 transition proceeds, the composition of interagency

leadership is likely to evolve. Pending final decisions on U.S. presence post-2014, disrupting the

financial links of the drug trade will remain critically important and will require the type of intelligence support currently provided by ATFC. The interagency is analyzing the possibility of integrating the ATFC into the IOCC for better coordination and collaboration.

Central Asian states have repeatedly expressed their concern over narco-traffickers and extremist networks operating across their irregular borders and extreme mountainous terrain and welcome DoD assistance in confronting these challenges. Given these countries' systemic lack of training, maintenance, and standardization, dating back to the Soviet era, DoD has provided modernized CN equipment, training, and facility investments. Working with DEA and other interagency partners, DoD has provided CN equipment and regional training in support to the Central Asian Regional Information Collection Center and is exploring further interagency opportunities to support the border management efforts. Programs funded with host-nation resources have been modeled after U.S. programs and have helped modernize many border crossing points. DoD efforts also provide additional leverage points for negotiating agreements to the Northern Distribution Network in support of the war effort in Afghanistan. These efforts are often the most consistent or only reliable assistance the U.S. government can provide in a timely manner, and they help maintain diplomatic relationships in a region where influence is difficult to maintain.

## DoD Post -2014 Strategy

DoD's Post-2014 *Strategy* prioritizes programs that disrupt, degrade, and dismantle illicit narcotics networks. DoD's primary focus remains sustaining and advancing Afghan CN capabilities while also continuing to work with Pakistani and Central Asian law enforcement agencies. The government of Afghanistan must be able to control narco-trafficking to advance the security of its population and allow room for lawful economic growth. The Strategy outlines three broad objectives: 1) to contain/reduce the flow of drugs from Afghanistan; 2) to disrupt and dismantle transnational criminal organizations; and 3) to reduce the flow of illicit proceeds that finance insurgent and terrorist activities globally.

Our CN strategy for post-2014 Afghanistan can be summarized by saying that we believe we must focus on three key areas:

1)      Continued support for vetted units,

2)      Continued aviation capacity building, and

3)      Continued leveraging of international and interagency capabilities.

First, specialized CN units have shown that they are willing and able to do the job, and more and more specialized-units are now able to plan, execute, and follow-through on CN missions on their own. For example, in December, the DoD-supported and DEA-mentored Sensitive Investigative Unit was able to use judicially authorized wire intercepts to build a case that led to the arrest of 2 criminals and the seizure of 660 grams of heroin, 500 boxes of ammunition, 40 remote control IEDs, and 75 rocket-propelled grenades.

Second, I cannot overstate how continued support to building Afghanistan's aviation capability is vital due to the terrain of Afghanistan. For any security effort, and certainly to run effective CN operations, Afghan forces must have adequate air mobility to operate in the remote areas where insurgents and illicit drug networks operate. My office's focus has been the SMW, which has demonstrated the capability to completely plan and execute operations without international assistance. With greater aviation capabilities over time, the SMW will be able to conduct vital operations, continue training aircrews in more complex operations, and focus more resources on further developing the capability of the Afghan maintenance team to independently maintain aircraft. That said, our experiences in Colombia and elsewhere illustrate that it can take a decade or more for an aviation capability to become truly self-sustaining. In a nation like Afghanistan where budgetary pressures will be high, it may take longer. With sustained support, however, we are confident the SMW can continue to make progress.

Third, as U.S. and coalition forces Afghanistan drawdown over the coming year, the interagency and international partnerships we have forged will become increasingly important as our military and other capabilities are reduced inside Afghanistan. The worldwide breadth of the Afghan heroin trade will require working across numerous "seams" between the Geographic Combatant Commands and building upon existing international partnerships to disrupt the flow of drugs and other illicit commodities. We are therefore working with several Combatant Commands, U.S. law enforcement agencies, U.S. intelligence agencies, and interested international partners to create a regional targeting and intelligence center able to coordinate and facilitate international efforts to disrupt the flow of heroin, target illicit sources of revenue, and dismantle criminal organizations that pose the greatest threat to U.S. and international security.

The regional center will help DoD retain the interagency and international collaboration that has been so effective for CN efforts in Afghanistan and the region and will bridge the seams of several Combatant Commands. The center will help fill the gap where space for personnel on the ground in Afghanistan is no longer available and will provide reach-back capability, intelligence/operations fusion capabilities, regional CN support, and regional counter threat finance support. We would begin by expanding upon the current Operation Riptide, located in Bahrain, which leverages the capabilities of U.S. and international law enforcement and national intelligence agencies to facilitate interdictions, seizures, investigations, and prosecutions. Naval interdictions from Combined Maritime Forces in Bahrain, notably by Canada's HMCS TORONTO and by Australia's HMAS MELBOURNE, have proven the international community's ability to identify, track, board, and seize illicit cargo on the high seas. HMCS TORONTO conducted seven seizures in 2013. We estimate that just one percent of the value of what they removed from the high seas is equal to the amount of funding necessary to outfit a platoon of insurgents. On January 17 of this year, acting on specific intelligence and in collaboration with the U.S. Naval Criminal Investigative Service, the TORONTO intercepted a dhow off the coast of Tanzania, seizing 280 kg of suspected heroin. A regional targeting center would allow us to retain valuable working relationships that enhance our ability to identify, track, board, and seize illicit cargo on the high seas and to expand our ability to attack these networks with law enforcement partners on land. It will require us to operate across combatant commands, which we believe is essential to effectively combat the global heroin trade.

Given the close association of drug trafficking with other national security threats such as terrorism, insurgency, and weapons trafficking, the authorities and expertise of our law enforcement partners are critical to helping the Department accomplish non-CN specific national security objectives as well. Having a flexible tool like our CN authorities and Central Transfer Account allows us to work with them to effectively meet both of our goals. This collaboration is a true win-win that helps the U.S. government remain effective in today's more austere budgetary environment.

In closing, DoD plans to continue its successful and effective partnership with the interagency and international partners to disrupt the sources of revenue for terrorists and insurgents, and reduce the corrosive, corruptive, and destabilizing impact of illicit narcotics. Our primary goal is to continue support and sustainment of Afghanistan's CN law enforcement institutions which have made tremendous progress over the course of Operation Enduring Freedom. DoD also expects that the establishment of a regional center will help counter the threat of narco-trafficking by providing a coordinated platform for our law enforcement and international partners and greater visibility into the illicit narcotics flow into the United States.

Thank you for the opportunity to talk about DoD's CN work in Afghanistan. I look forward to your questions and comments.

---

Ms. ROS-LEHTINEN. Thank you very much, and I agree about the importance of those DEA wire intercept centers. We toured the facility and it was very, very impressive.

Last year, as we know, we saw a significant increase in poppy cultivation to record levels which is a huge setback to our efforts to cut off that link between extremist groups and the drug trade. The vast majority of poppy is cultivated in some of the most dangerous, least secure areas of Afghanistan operated and controlled by the Taliban and other extremists. Which U.S. Government agency is in charge of coordination efforts for counternarcotics programs in Afghanistan? I'll let you ponder that one.

Also, the drawdown has already caused our agencies to decrease their staffs and their presence in Afghanistan and we still don't know what the post-2014 footprint will be. This uncertainty affects more than just our military presence, but it impacts our strategic goals that we're aiming to accomplish in Afghanistan, including counternarcotics efforts.

How heavily does the uncertainty about this post-2014 decision weigh over our plans for future counternarcotics efforts? How effective can we be with a minimal to perhaps zero troop presence?

Mr. Capra, you testified that sustaining successful security transition to Afghan forces will rest, in part, on limiting insurgent's access to drug-related funding and the support that they get. And in response to this challenge, DEA reopened the Kabul country office. At its peak, DEA had 97 authorized positions in Afghanistan plus a number of contract employees. Did DEA receive the proper number of staff that you requested from the Embassy? And, if not, why not? And we're now entrusting the Afghan counternarcotics forces to do a job that is arguably tougher now than it was before, and they will have less U.S. support with which to do it. We've made remarkable progress in training their forces, that is true, but I'm not sure that they have the capability to handle this very serious threat to both Afghan and U.S. national security.

SIGAR in a 2009 audit has criticized INL for Counternarcotics Justice Center. Secretary Brownfield, what are your thoughts about the audit, and what is the current capacity of the Afghan forces for counternarcotics operations? Thank you.

Ambassador BROWNFIELD. I'll start, Madam Chairman, and pass the DEA staffing question, obviously, to the good Dr. Capra seated to my side.

All of the questions are excellent. Let me try to knock off the three that I believe most directly apply to me. First question, who is responsible for coordinating strategy and drug policy in Afghanistan? Madam Chairman, we have an interagency U.S. Government strategy that was blessed through the White House-managed interagency process in 2012 and produced in December of that year.

Since that time, the three organizations represented at this table, DoD, DEA, and INL have all done our own review and developed our own modifications and adjustments based upon the expectation that 2014 is a transition year. And we have attempted to answer the question for our individual agencies where will we be going post-2014 in terms of our drug efforts? Who is responsible for coordinating in the field in Afghanistan? Probably, I'm the closest to the stucky in this regard. It is the United States Ambassador, but he expects his INL director to pull together at least in some sort of strategic and policy way all of those players who are working the drug issue in Afghanistan.

The 2014 and beyond footprint. You put your finger right on the issue, Madam Chairman. Everyone at this table would like to know with great precision how many people will we have available for this mission after 2014. And the truth of the matter is we still do not know. This falls into the category of those variables I was talking about in my statement.

We do not know what is the nature of the security relationship, whether we will have a BSA and what it will say, who will win the election in April of this year, what will be the number of resources that are available to us out of the FY 2013 and the FY 2014 appropriations bill, and what the other international players will be doing. We are obligated, you pay us to put together the best possible set of policies and programs that allow us to adjust to whatever those variables eventually deliver.

Finally, thank you for the question on the Counternarcotics Justice Center. In a hearing across the way about 3 or 4 weeks ago I did hear from the Special Inspector General for Afghanistan Reconstruction comments in terms of the CNJC. They surprised me because they were almost 180 degrees different from my own perspective. I believe the CNJC is one of the great success stories of counternarcotics in Afghanistan today.

When I was there a week ago, I inaugurated a new detention facility at that Justice Center for one simple reason. They are investigating and prosecuting so many cases that they did not have enough detention space to hold the accused during the process of the trial. And we needed to build an annex. They are investigating well, prosecuting well. They have a conviction rate in the high 90s. It is widely regarded as one of the success stories of Afghanistan and, in fact, there are a number of other elements of the Justice sector that are hoping that they could mimic or do a similar operation to the CNJC. Dr. Capra, over to you.

Mr. CAPRA. That's why I like having meetings with Ambassador Brownfield.

Madam Chair, a couple of questions you raised. First and foremost, our footprint. Obviously, when we started there was at 97. What I'd like to do is talk about first and foremost, we, DEA, would not have the ability to operate there without the funding that we get from Department of State and DoD. Nearly this year, Fiscal Year 2013, $30.5 million from Ambassador Brownfield I like to call it, another close to $15 million from DoD. We spend, DEA's direct appropriations, $17 million for 13 positions, three pilots, and three fast teams, but in order to operate we would have needed a lot more personnel than we did. Now, this year comes in, we know that the U.S. Government drawdown is going to impact everybody. We got asked if we're pulling out of forward operating bases just like the military did. What's our plan for the future when we're looking at Afghanistan? And this is never done in a vacuum, meeting with our interagency partners, as well. So, what we do just like you're familiar with any other part of the world where DEA operates whether it's South America or Europe is we get the biggest bang out of our buck with our SIUs and our NIUs. It's a gold standard anywhere in the world so with effective vetting and standing these teams up, training with our people, so in a combat theater we were pushing out with them constantly, so we knew that was going to be less and less likely. So, how could we operate in that region? We put a plan together with certain assumptions that have to be in place. One is funding, are we able to have continued funding?

The next certainly is security, the security of our men and women there, as well. So, all that goes into, and I don't want to rehash what Ambassador Brownfield said, but it is, we're not sure what's going to happen. But we are moving toward a drawdown, and by the end of this year we will probably have somewhere around 47 people in country. That includes still rotating fast members there once a quarter. And really the crux of what we're doing there is building capacity and capability of the Afghan Counternarcotics Police. They're the vetted teams, and having them to be able to stand on their own, and in some instances, or actually a lot of instances they're doing that right now.

In this past year, they've done over 2,400 operations, 2,400. They've arrested over 2,200 individuals, they've seized over 121 tons of narcotics and another 32,000 kilos of chemicals. And that's not including the typical weapons and hardware, communications hardware, IED making materials that are out there. So, when you ask, and the right thing is to ask sometimes is what is—we started with nothing when we got there. We started with nothing, and here we've developed SIs, NIs, TIs, judicial wire intercept program which you know is critical anywhere in the world. And then we have to look at it from a regional approach, too. What will happen? So we're not sitting here waiting and saying okay, we're also looking at being able to partner with our regional partners in the region in Central Asia, all a part of the plan.

Ms. ROS-LEHTINEN. Thank you.

Mr. CAPRA. Thank you, ma'am.

Ms. ROS-LEHTINEN. And, Ms. Logan, if you have anything to add.

Ms. LOGAN. The only thing I would add is, you know, most of the places where we do our counternarcotics work are not U.S. declared war zones, so this is about us transitioning, as well, to using some of the strategies and the approaches we've used elsewhere.

It will be more difficult, Madam Chair. You're exactly right. I mean, it's a very hard problem. And we always see ebbs and flows, and so while I think all of us don't dispute the sort of facts on the ground, I think how you interpret them, as my colleague said, we see a lot of new but really impressive capability. Is it enough? Will it answer the question, you know, the issues the country is going to face in the next 10 years? Probably not enough, it's not going to solve the whole problem, but we can still keep and grow that capability. And the country itself, I mean, we've seen a lot of evidence that the people of Afghanistan do not want to be a narco state. This is not something they're comfortable with, so we have a lot of material to work with, but we will transition to something that is more similar to what we do around the globe as opposed to what we've been able to do in Afghanistan.

Ms. ROS-LEHTINEN. Thank you so much, and thank you for the committee members putting up with how long I went on that. Mr. Deutch, you're recognized.

Mr. DEUTCH. Thank you, Madam Chairman.

Ms. Logan, you said in your testimony, you gave one example of the Sensitive Investigative Unit that used judicially authorized wire intercepts to build the case that led to the arrest of two criminals, seizure of 660 grams of heroin, 500 boxes of ammunition, 40 remote control IEDs and 75 rocket propelled grenades.

Where do these RPGs come from, and where are the huge increase in arms that the narcoterrorists use, where do they come from?

Ms. LOGAN. Without getting into too many specifics, I would say, you know, a concern that DoD has across the board and certainly in this region is that the same networks that move drugs move everything else. So, we see links in these networks, we certainly see flow.

One of the goals we have with this potential regional cell that we'd like to pull back into the Gulf to give some reach back ability is to get greater fidelity on some of those networks. As I mentioned, we've seen a lot of things going from the Mokran coast which is both Iran and Pakistan that flow actually into Africa, but we see it flowing out of Africa to the rest of the world. We see things going through the neighboring countries and into Afghanistan from neighboring countries, so we are increasingly concerned about trying to develop not just the CN approach but a counter network approach because these networks are linked. They're not all the same, but they have linkages and they have vulnerabilities that we are trying to explore.

Mr. DEUTCH. Who do you work with as you take that network approach, because if—and, certainly, the goal is—I mean, if at the same time we can address the narcotics and heroin, but also tackle RPGs and the tremendous flow of weapons we need to do that. Who do you work with——

Ms. LOGAN. It's very much an interagency effort along with international. I mean, the British are side by side with us in all of this. As you know, our Joint Improvised Explosive Deice Defeat Organization, the JIEDDO has led on specifically finding the networks that move the arms and the precursors for that. And then we try to overlap that in country and back here. Actually, multiple commands for DoD, it's not just Central Command but COCOM, Central Operations Command also tries to draw that fusion. And then all of us using our partners, DEA, State Department, FBI, other law—you know, we really try to take a very holistic view of understanding—Treasury is a huge partner for us in all of these sort of network attack strategies and trying to map that out.

Mr. DEUTCH. Okay, great. Thanks. I appreciate that.

The U.N. Office on Drugs and Crime estimates that 90 metric tons of heroin travels from Afghanistan through Central Asia, worth about $750 million. Can you discuss our operations? I'll actually open this to the panel, our operations with Afghanistan's neighbors on stemming the flow of drugs through their countries all throughout Central Asia, in particular Russia, the endpoint for much of Afghanistan's originating narcotics for trade routes through Central Asia, Iran for shipments headed west, Pakistan for shipments headed east. Can you describe those relationships and those efforts, Ambassador Brownfield?

Ambassador BROWNFIELD. I'll start, Congressman, and then yield the floor after I've offered my input.

We began a systematic and structured effort to develop a regional program that involved the five Central Asian Republics which yes, I can name; Kazakhstan, Krgyzstan, Uzbekistan, Tajikstan, and Turkmenistan. Thank you very much. Plus Afghanistan, the Russian Federation, and ourselves. And the objective was to develop an initiative that would tie them all together in some way with the same database, the same information, the ability to coordinate operations.

I launched this effort in 2011 with a trip to the region and we called it the Central Asia Counternarcotics Initiative, or CACI. It has not yet been a resounding success, and I clearly misread several signals. One signal was the extent to which the five Central Asian nations are comfortable cooperating with one another. And I discovered that, in fact, I thought there was more enthusiasm for that than there really was.

Second, I misread what I thought would be a very attractive offer for the large nation to the north to give them access to intelligence and operations in real time that was happening in Afghanistan and allow them to influence. And, in fact, found they were not as enthusiastic about that as I hoped they would be. So, the initiative is still on the books. We still have a concept and are making step by step progress.

We have—we are working with an organization that would serve as the coordinating center called CARICC or the Central Asia Regional Information Coordination Center. We are working with the United Nations organization that does drugs, UNODC to provide training for specialized units. We are moving in the right direction, we're not there yet. Dr. C.

Mr. CAPRA. Congressman, thank you. Again, part of the strategy that we have is to be able to look at a counternarcotics strategy on a regional approach. So to follow on with Ambassador Brownfield, what we're looking at is the Central Asian states, as well, including high-level talks with Russia to exchange information back and forth. A lot of this heroin that's leaving the country is going into the hands of Russian organized crime and the like. So, to dialogue with those Central Asian states where some of the offices—we have offices in some of them, and in some of the offices, as Ambassador Brownfield said, it's a little bit more challenging as we're working there, but the object is before we were even there we had this containment type of strategy in the region to address what was going on there. And it's to follow through with that, it's to take a look at the regional approach, it's continuing to dialogue knowing full well that we're going to drawdown, you have to be able to do that.

Mr. DEUTCH. Can I have 30 more seconds, Madam Chairman? Thank you. I appreciate the efforts and I understand having recently spent time in the region, as well, that your assessment I think is accurate about the way that the countries interact with one another. But I'd just like to know whether each of those countries individually, do you believe that each of the countries on their own is committed to this effort?

Ambassador BROWNFIELD. Sure, the tough questions you always defer to me, Dr. Capra.

The answer, as is usually the case when you're talking about a number of countries, Congressman, is some yes, some less yes for a variety of reasons. One or more country might feel that somehow it is separate from this problem and, therefore, they don't have to address it as intensely as others. Some may see that they have a national interest perhaps in trying to either absorb some of this traffic or direct it in some other way. Some are undoubtedly playing some degree of regional politics in terms of what they will do or what they will not do. They all have a common interest. To my knowledge, no serious democratic or even remotely democratic government in the world wants to become a narco state, a country who's government is dominated or controlled by narcotics trafficking organizations. They all have that common interest. A couple of the seven are moving at a faster speed than others, and I think I'd answer your question that way.

Mr. DEUTCH. I appreciate it and I know my time is up. I'm heartened by the approach that focuses on networks and just not only on CN. It is true they don't want to become narco states, but it's also true that through these networks the spread of arms through their states and those who possess the arms is another major consideration they should have in working together with us and with each other to try to address this. I thank the panel very much.

Ms. ROS-LEHTINEN. Thank you, Mr. Deutch. Mr. Weber, you're up.

Mr. WEBER. Thank you. Ambassador, I noticed you rattled off about five countries, Tajikstan, Uzbekistan, Pakistan, why don't you take a stan. I wasn't sure what all they were. Can you go back through those again?

Ambassador BROWNFIELD. If that's a challenge, Congressman, I certainly can, thank you very much. I said Kazakhstan, Krgyzstan, Uzbekistan, Tajikstan, and Turkmenistan. That is KKUTT, and those are the five Central Asian Republics.

Mr. WEBER. Okay. I'm looking at it on a map. Okay. Golly. And I don't know who this question is for. Afghanistan is a narco state. Does the DEA, do we have a track record of coming into a situation like this before and being able to clean it up, or is this a first?

Mr. CAPRA. Congressman, Afghanistan is a completely different theater as a combat theater, so it presented a whole bunch of new challenges. There are, I would submit, there are some similarities in places around the world that when we first started, for instance, when I first started as a young agent in New York, we never thought——

Mr. WEBER. New York was the battleground?

Mr. CAPRA. Pretty much, it was part of it.

Mr. WEBER. Oh, you mean a different country.

Mr. CAPRA. So we looked at Colombia at a time and said would we ever be able to work with Colombia. That's 27 years ago. I just was down in Colombia again. Colombia has been and is——

Mr. WEBER. Yes, but it wasn't in civil war, and it wasn't as desolate as this is.

Mr. CAPRA. No, no, and I'm not suggesting—and there was a government there, but the narcotics trade had taken hold of Colombia. And if we remember, you had cartels attacking the Supreme Court killing judges. So, yes, I'm not trying to make both comparisons, but you said what is it? Well, we decided to hang in there, Plan Colombia took effect. Now we have countries like Algeria that go to Colombia to learn about best practices in counternarcotics.

Mr. WEBER. Okay. Well, of course, I realize Colombia is how many hours away by plane?

Mr. CAPRA. From here we can get there pretty quickly.

Mr. WEBER. I mean, 4 or 5 hours.

Mr. CAPRA. Five hours.

Mr. WEBER. And that's not the case in Afghanistan.

Mr. CAPRA. No, sir. No, sir.

Mr. WEBER. So, in Afghanistan, I don't know who this question is for, who is your best ally in cleaning this up? Is it the Afghanistan Government?

Mr. CAPRA. For our best ally it's the law enforcement component which is the Counternarcotics Police in Afghanistan.

Mr. WEBER. And——

Mr. CAPRA. It is—I'm sorry, go ahead.

Mr. WEBER. No corruption there?

Mr. CAPRA. We face corruption everywhere, but let me go right into that, because that's one of the challenges that we face not just there but anywhere. Narcotics trade engenders lots of money, engenders corruption. It just does. Since our SIUs were stood up, these are our Sensitive Investigative Units, our Narcotics Investigative Unit which is the action arm, since they've been set up we have conducted in the past year alone, there have been over 700 individuals that have been convicted. Of them, of those convictions, 50 of them have been government officials.

Mr. WEBER. Okay, and that leads me to my next question. So, when you go in to accuse somebody, arrest somebody, detain, whatever, they have a constitution in Afghanistan?

Mr. CAPRA. To the——

Mr. WEBER. So, you all operate within the parameters of their constitution.

Mr. CAPRA. The Afghan law, that's right. We leave it—right, exactly. Exactly.

Mr. WEBER. Okay.

Mr. CAPRA. Now, we're doing things jointly, they are bilateral investigations so DEA is conducting investigations alongside our partners.

Mr. WEBER. Okay.

Mr. CAPRA. In some instances we've indicted groups here in the United States, as well. But the Afghans are using their justice system to convict, and they've got a pretty significant—it's not perfect and I get that, but we're talking about a conviction rate of over 90 percent.

Mr. WEBER. Okay.

Mr. CAPRA. So, we're again, when you look back say what did you start with?

Mr. WEBER. Do you all have, does the DEA, does our drug interdiction forces, do they have prosecute—I don't know—immunity? I mean, if they make a mistake, I know there was some discussion about the Afghanistan leaving people there. Were you all part of that?

Mr. CAPRA. I'm not sure what——

Mr. WEBER. In other words, they were saying that—Karzai, I think, wouldn't agree to the—there was some kind of immunity that was going to be granted.

Mr. CAPRA. I'll turn it over to you.

Mr. WEBER. Am I misremembering, Ambassador?

Ambassador BROWNFIELD. Congressman, on a case by case basis there may be matters of immunity, for example, sitting members of the national legislature.

Mr. WEBER. What I'm saying is if as a DEA agent you got there and you hurt somebody in your line of work. Are you protected as long as you acted in good faith?

Ambassador BROWNFIELD. All U.S. Government personnel in Afghanistan today either operate under a version of the Status of Forces Agreement that covers military personnel, or if they report up to the Chief of Mission, to the United States Ambassador, they have diplomatic protection. And to that extent they have a degree of immunity.

Mr. WEBER. Gotcha. Mr. Capra, you said 121 tons, I think you seized 32,000 tons of chemical, and I did a little research on Afghanistan, 31 or 2 million people and they're not exactly thriving industrial complexes. Where are they getting—who's supplying them?

Mr. CAPRA. Well, they're getting chemicals from different parts of the world. They're using—these are rudimentary places out in the middle of the desert that they're—but the narcotics trade is funding the insurgency.

Mr. WEBER. Okay.

Mr. CAPRA. And those drugs or those finished products are leaving Afghanistan and some are being used there by the population.

Mr. WEBER. Okay. And I notice if I could tell on my map on my iPad, it looked like it had a tiny, tiny border with China, Afghanistan does. How many miles is that, do you know?

Mr. CAPRA. I'd defer to the Ambassador.

Ambassador BROWNFIELD. It's a very—the part that actually borders on China is minuscule. What it is, it's a little corridor. You'll see from your map, it's called the Panjshir Valley, and it's about 100 miles long, and I'm guessing the actual border with China is maybe something as small as 10 or 15 miles.

Mr. WEBER. Okay. Are you seeing drug trade going in and out of China?

Ambassador BROWNFIELD. I do not think we are, Congressman, not out of Afghanistan. China, we believe, does have a growing drug consumption and abuse problem which is logical as its economy grows and it develops a middle class. Our sense is that most of the Chinese market is supplied out of Burma/Myanmar and not out of Afghanistan.

Mr. WEBER. And final question, forgive me, Madam Chair. What country would you say is our greatest ally in this fight, not counting Afghanistan? And what country is our biggest deterrent in this fight?

Ambassador BROWNFIELD. I could define that in dozens, if not hundreds of ways, Congressman. I will define it this way. The country that has been most willing to serve as an ally and a partner with us, to offer up resources and personnel and to jointly staff our programs, projects would be the United Kingdom, would be the British. I would give them the highest credit in that regard.

I'm not sure how to define who would be the worst. I mean, among others the worst would be those who are not participating at all, and that's probably about 180 countries around the world.

Mr. WEBER. Well, clearly, you said Russia had organized crime, and they were going to Russia. So, if you could just choose a list of top three, if you could just mitigate with a magic wand the top three countries and get them uninvolved, would Russia be number one?

Ambassador BROWNFIELD. Yes, although——

Mr. WEBER. But I don't want to put you on the spot, but I mean to put you on the spot.

Ambassador BROWNFIELD. I mean, if you were to ask me would it be helpful if Russian citizens ceased using Afghan heroin, yes, it would. And I believe the Russian Government would agree with that, as well. They also have the objective of attacking their own heroin abuse problem.

We could say the same thing about both of their—of Afghanistan's neighbors to the west and to the east, Iran and Pakistan are major consumers of the product, as well. And I don't want to make judgment calls on those two governments, but I have every reason to believe that they also would like to reduce the amount of heroin that their citizens are consuming.

It's a complicated process, as you well know. It is not possible to deal with the drug issue in Afghanistan and say if we just solve this one issue, cultivation, or interdiction, or laboratories, or precursor chemicals, if we just solve one issue we have solved the problem. We have to solve all elements of the problem to some extent. That's the lesson we learned over 20 or 30 years in Colombia. When you finally focus on all elements of the problem you do deliver a long-term solution.

Mr. WEBER. Thank you, Madam Chair.

Ms. ROS-LEHTINEN. Thank you, excellent set of questions. Ms. Frankel, you are our clean up batter. Make it good.

Ms. FRANKEL. Well, thank you, Madam Chair. As a junior member I often feel like I'm a character in the Agatha Christie novel, "And Then There Were None." And I also want to say for the record that——

Ms. ROS-LEHTINEN. Means that you're the criminal then?

Ms. FRANKEL. I don't know what that means.

Ms. ROS-LEHTINEN. I don't know.

Ms. FRANKEL. Just for the record, Madam Chair, you and I are wearing red today with the other women in the Congress because today is in honor of the American Heart Association.

Ms. ROS-LEHTINEN. And we have to run over there as soon as you're done.

Ms. FRANKEL. That's right.

Ms. ROS-LEHTINEN. Okay.

Ms. FRANKEL. Heart disease kills more women than any other illness.

Anyway, getting back to Afghanistan, I have a couple of questions. So, according to the data sheet that we received it says that the opium production in 2013 was equivalent to approximately 4 percent of Afghanistan's gross domestic product. So, can you just give me a general idea of what the other 96 percent is?

Ambassador BROWNFIELD. I don't claim to be an expert on the Afghan economy, Congresswoman. I would say that Afghanistan is still largely a rural country, so I would speculate that probably more than 50 percent of its gross domestic product is still agricultural produce of some sort. They have a limited amount of what I would call small level industrial and manufacturing, and they have some degree of minerals and mining. Beyond that, I think what you would see in Afghanistan is the economy you would expect from a country that's in—in terms of gross domestic product and per capita, GDP, probably in the bottom 5 percent of the nations of the world.

Ms. FRANKEL. So, the farmers who are producing the opium—is most of the direct toward the Taliban, or other illicit—what we call an illicit group, rather than for the general well-being of Afghani population?

Ambassador BROWNFIELD. That's a terrific question and one, obviously, in which we have to be somewhat speculative since, as you well can imagine, farmers who are producing opium poppy and selling the poppy do not report either the sales or their motivation to any government organizations or offices.

My own sense in Afghanistan, as by the way in most of the world where you find subsistence level farmers who are cultivating and selling an illicit drug, whether it's cocoa leaf in Latin America or opium poppy in Central Asia or Southeast Asia, and Burma and Myanmar is that the farmers themselves are subsistence level farmers. They are trying to make a basic living for their families. They are not inherently criminals. They are not even politically motivated and what they are trying to do. They conclude that they can make $500 a year if they grow wheat, but they can make $2,000 a year if they grow opium poppy, so they grow opium poppy.

Now, they then sell it, and they sell it either to a terrorist type organization such as the Taliban, and thereby allow the Taliban to in a sense become the producer, the trafficker, and earn the real rewards because the subsistence farmer is not making a great deal, or they sell it to a traditional criminal organization.

At the end of the day, that's where the Taliban, in essence, gets its revenue by selecting the regions where it has a substantial presence, where there is minimal security provided by the government, and either intimidating and forcing the farmers to cultivate and sell to them, or simply become the buyer of the product. That I would suggest is probably what we see in Afghanistan, just as I would suggest it's what you see in Colombia, Peru, or Bolivia with your subsistence farmer.

Ms. FRANKEL. So, one of the focuses here is alternative development. And you feel like it is possible to provide them with some alternative that would keep them from growing opium?

Ambassador BROWNFIELD. Yes, Congresswoman, you put your finger right on what, obviously, has to be one of the elements of a program. And Jimmy Capra talked about interdiction which is absolutely essential, as is investigations, laboratory take downs, money laundering and so forth, but we have to address the problem, as well, at its opening on the chain, and that is cultivation.

We have developed over the last 10 years three programs that are designed to address this issue, one that we call Governor-Led Eradication. It's a very simple program. We pay the governor of a province $250 for each hectare of opium poppy, that's 2.5 acres roughly, that the province eradicates. If they don't eradicate, they don't get paid. If they eradicate 1,000, they get $250,000. Simple, hard to cheat on that. We count up what was eradicated and we then pay them.

The second program is what we call the Good Performers Initiative. This is a program again with the governors in the provinces where we reach an understanding or a contract, and we say if you eradicate X number of hectares, let's say 5,000 hectares, what we will offer for you is two schools, three clinics, four new roads, and an electricity grid that will address these two or three villages. Again, it's a good program because you can't cheat. First they eradicate, then the benefits flow into the province.

The third program is directly on point for what you're describing, alternative development. This is the Helmand Food Zone that Mr. Deutch was talking about, and what I hope will become in the course of later this year the Kandahar Food Zone. This is where we will offer again together with the governors and the local government, and the Ministry of Counternarcotics direct alternative development assistance, not just a barrel of seeds so they can plant wheat instead of opium poppy but, in fact, the technology, the equipment, a road system that allows them to get their product to market, and general improvements in their villages that allow them to have a stake in their future. This is what the Food Zone project is all about.

It's expensive, Congresswoman. That's why as we were addressing the realities of 2014 and beyond we have a flexible program that allows us to move from province to province. We don't have the resources to do it everywhere at the same time. We're not going to have those resources. I think we agree with that. We do have the resources to say the toughest area right now is Kandahar, for example, so we will do a Food Zone in Kandahar. We'll work it for 2 years, then we will see where the next target zone is, and move there. That's how we're trying to address the issue.

Ms. FRANKEL. Madam Chair, may I ask——

Ms. ROS-LEHTINEN. Absolutely, yes.

Ms. FRANKEL. Since it's just the three of us here. I think many of us have been very disturbed about what's happened to funds that we've—that's gone into Afghanistan, in military and in USAID, a lot of corruption, a lot of waste, a lot of fraud, all that. So, a question I have for you is how could we be certain that if we inject more resources into the kind of activities you're describing that we're not going to have the same waste, fraud, and corruption? And that's one part of the question.

The other one is how much of the money do you think that has flowed into Afghanistan, the billions of dollars through the U.S. Government, has already gone into producing opium?

Ambassador BROWNFIELD. I'm not sure how to answer that question. I would say certainly none of the money that we have provided has gone into programs designed to produce opium, but I'm sure that's not your question. Let me answer——

Ms. FRANKEL. Well, through corruption, waste, fraud, something is happening to some of that money.

Ambassador BROWNFIELD. And at the end of the day, I'm not going to be able to give you a good figure or even an estimate for Afghanistan at large since I, obviously, only do the counternarcotics part of it.

I will tell you, however, that I feel pretty confident about the programs that we are managing with DEA, in particular, on counternarcotics for the following reason. For the most part, when we provide direct funding to the Government of Afghanistan, it is for acts that have already occurred and been verified which is to say what they have already eradicated, or what they have already interdicted, or what they have already taken down in terms of labs.

In terms of the support that we're providing for the Special Units through DEA, DEA is working directly with them day in, day out, sometimes 24 hours a day. They've got very good visibility in terms of what they're doing, and they are vetted, which is to say assessed on a regular basis to determine whether any of the individuals have been corrupted or penetrated.

Ms. FRANKEL. Well, what about through USAID? Isn't that one of the purposes was to have—was on economic redevelopment?

Ambassador BROWNFIELD. Sure, and I have to defer on giving you an answer there because, obviously, I cannot speak for USAID.

Ms. FRANKEL. Is it just us, can I ask one more then? That's it, one more.

Mr. DEUTCH. My friend and neighbor from Florida has——

Ms. FRANKEL. Yes. So, what is your—any of you can answer this. In terms of the danger of the narcotic issue here in Afghanistan, do you see it—is it more of a health, more of terrorism-related? What do you think is the largest danger?

Ms. LOGAN. Ma'am, I think we in DoD see it as genuinely a national security threat that will continue. As I mentioned this, and as was mentioned by my colleagues, the amount of money and the use of those funds by our adversaries for multiple nefarious purposes, this is not—it is tragic the actual usage issues, of course. We're all very saddened by that, and Afghanistan is facing a growing problem itself, but for us it's really about what else this pays for, and the instability and corruption that it breeds, as well, that makes it impossible for the people of that region and many other regions to reach their full potential to be honest. But it's a national security question for us. It really very much fundamentally is, and I let my colleagues answer, too.

Mr. CAPRA. Just very quickly, ma'am, the narcotics trade generates billions of dollars, and those billions of dollars have the ability to destabilize not just neighborhoods but entire nations, especially those who are prone to weakness and corruption. They have the ability to fund extremist groups around the world, political organizations, and that's what we see that's going on there in Afghanistan. That's the threat of that narcotics trade. Mr. Ambassador.

Ambassador BROWNFIELD. Well, I'll close it, Congresswoman, by saying three things. There are three threats out there. One, one of the world's largest terrorist organizations receives most of its domestic funding from narcotics. That's the Taliban and that's the Afghan heroin industry. Second, it represents a threat to the stability, and for that matter future of democracy in Afghanistan. We have invested a substantial amount of U.S. national effort in that nation. One could argue that it is in our interest to ensure that it does not become a victim to drug trafficking. And third and finally, you can argue about the number. I've heard figures between 4 and 7 percent of U.S. heroin consumed in the United States is of Afghan origin, but there's absolutely no reason why that couldn't surge. There's nothing magical that keeps Afghan heroin from coming to the United States, and if that happens it is a direct threat to the people and communities of the United States of America.

Ms. FRANKEL. Thank you. Mr. Deutch, I just have one last question, which is then which is the agency that you would designate to do the alternative redevelopment work?

Ambassador BROWNFIELD. It would be between me from the INL side and USAID. USAID does rural development. Now, they are the ones who work with farmers and farming programs. I do the drug programs. It is my responsibility to lay out the infrastructure, if you will, for an alternative development program, and USAID can and, in fact, very effectively does in Afghanistan the alternative development part of it.

You ask legitimate questions about diversion and corruption, but I do hold to my position that what USAID is doing in alternative development is, in fact, having impact where it is applied.

Mr. DEUTCH. Anything further, Congresswoman Frankel? With that, I thank——

Ms. FRANKEL. If you did ask, I do have one more. I'm taking advantage——

Mr. DEUTCH. You're taking advantage of——

Ms. FRANKEL. Yes. I don't know whether you can answer this question, but in our last budget I believe we reduced the USAID budget by half, so I'm just curious what you think that will have on effect what you're trying to do?

Ambassador BROWNFIELD. Congresswoman, let me tell you, you not only reduced USAID's suggested budget by half, you reduced everyone's budget for foreign assistance in Afghanistan by half, including my own. Now, you didn't write it into the law, you may recall. You may not have reread the 1,500 pages of the FY 14 Appropriations Bill yet. It was written as a statement of the managers of the bill, but it does, in fact, suggest 50 percent. And we're going to have to work our way through that issue. We in the Executive Branch, you in the United States Congress, we're going to have to talk about it. We're going to have to determine to what extent does this reflect the strong will of the United States Congress. And then we from our perspective have to say to you what the impact is going to be if we walk down this road. I think we have a great deal of conversation ahead of us on this issue before we reach final understanding as to how we're going to proceed.

Mr. DEUTCH. The gentle lady yields the balance of her time.

With that, I thank the witnesses for their patience, for their testimony today and for their service to the country. And that concludes the hearing, we're adjourned.

[Whereupon, at 4:17 p.m., the subcommittee was adjourned.]

# APPENDIX

---

MATERIAL SUBMITTED FOR THE RECORD

# SUBCOMMITTEE HEARING NOTICE
# COMMITTEE ON FOREIGN AFFAIRS
U.S. HOUSE OF REPRESENTATIVES
WASHINGTON, DC 20515-6128

### Subcommittee on the Middle East and North Africa
### Ileana Ros-Lehtinen (R-FL), Chairman

January 21, 2014

## TO:   MEMBERS OF THE COMMITTEE ON FOREIGN AFFAIRS

You are respectfully requested to attend an OPEN hearing of the Committee on Foreign Affairs to be held by the Subcommittee on the Middle East and North Africa, to be held in Room 2172 of the Rayburn House Office Building (and available live on the Committee website at www.foreignaffairs.house.gov):

**DATE:**            Wednesday, February 5, 2014

**TIME:**            2:00 p.m.

**SUBJECT:**         U.S. Counternarcotics Operations in Afghanistan

**WITNESSES:**       The Honorable William R. Brownfield
                     Assistant Secretary of State
                     Bureau of International Narcotics and Law Enforcement Affairs
                     U.S. Department of State

                     Mr. James L. Capra
                     Chief of Operations
                     U.S. Drug Enforcement Administration

                     Ms. Erin Logan
                     Principal Director for Counternarcotics and Global Threats
                     Office of the Under Secretary of Defense
                     U.S. Department of Defense

### By Direction of the Chairman

*The Committee on Foreign Affairs seeks to make its facilities accessible to persons with disabilities. If you are in need of special accommodations, please call 202/225-5021 at least four business days in advance of the event, whenever practicable. Questions with regard to special accommodations in general (including availability of Committee materials in alternative formats and assistive listening devices) may be directed to the Committee.*

# COMMITTEE ON FOREIGN AFFAIRS

MINUTES OF SUBCOMMITTEE ON _____ *Middle East and North Africa* _____ HEARING

Day__ *Wednesday*__ Date_____ *02/05/14*_____ Room_____ *2172*_____

Starting Time ___ *3:00 p.m.* ___ Ending Time ___ *4:15 p.m.* ___

Recesses _____ (____to ____) (____to ____) (____to ____) (____to ____) (____to ____) (____to ____)

**Presiding Member(s)**

*Chairman Ros-Lehtinen*

*Check all of the following that apply:*

Open Session ☑                                Electronically Recorded (taped) ☑
Executive (closed) Session ☐          Stenographic Record ☑
Televised ☑

**TITLE OF HEARING:**

*U.S. Counternarcotics Operations in Afghanistan*

**SUBCOMMITTEE MEMBERS PRESENT:**

*(See attendance sheet)*

**NON-SUBCOMMITTEE MEMBERS PRESENT:** *(Mark with an * if they are not members of full committee.)*

**HEARING WITNESSES:** Same as meeting notice attached? Yes ☑ No ☐
*(If "no", please list below and include title, agency, department, or organization.)*

**STATEMENTS FOR THE RECORD:** *(List any statements submitted for the record.)*

*None submitted*

**TIME SCHEDULED TO RECONVENE** _____
or
**TIME ADJOURNED** ___ *4:15 p.m.* ___

_____
Subcommittee Staff Director

**Hearing Attendance**

Hearing Title: U.S. Counternarcotics Operations in Afghanistan

Date: 02/05/14

*Noncommittee Members*

| Member | Present |
|---|---|
| Ros-Lehtinen, Ileana (FL) | X |
| Chabot, Steve (OH) | |
| Wilson, Joe (SC) | |
| Kinzinger, Adam (IL) | |
| Cotton, Tom (AR) | X |
| Weber, Randy (TX) | X |
| Desantis, Ron (FL) | |
| Collins, Doug (GA) | X |
| Meadows, Mark (NC) | |
| Yoho, Ted (FL) | |
| Messer, Luke (IN) | X |

| Member | Present |
|---|---|
| Deutch, Ted (FL) | X |
| Connolly, Gerald (VA) | X |
| Higgins, Brian (NY) | |
| Cicilline, David (RI) | X |
| Grayson, Alan (FL) | |
| Vargas, Juan (CA) | |
| Schneider, Bradley (IL) | |
| Kennedy, Joseph (MA) | |
| Meng, Grace (NY) | X |
| Frankel, Lois (FL) | X |